W9-BBD-902

Whole Food for Your Family

Foreword by **Melissa Urban**, co-creator of the Whole30

Whole Food for Your Family

100+ SIMPLE, BUDGET-FRIENDLY MEALS

Autumn Michaelis

creator of

MARINER BOOKS

Boston New York

HarperCollins books may be purchased for educational, business, or sales promotional use. For information, please email the Special Markets Department at SPsales@harpercollins.com.

FIRST EDITION

Designed by Toni Tajima
Interior Lifestyle Photographs © 2021 by Lacey Carney
Back Panel Author Photograph © 2021 by Kylie Astle
30-minute meal, airfryer, and nut-free icons by Imagination lol/Shutterstock.com
Freezer-friendly icon by AVIcon/Shutterstock.com
Egg-free icon by Crunchyyy/Shutterstock.com

Library of Congress Cataloging-in-Publication Data has been applied for.

ISBN 978-0-358-61530-9

22 23 24 25 26 RTL 10 9 8 7 6 5 4 3 2 1

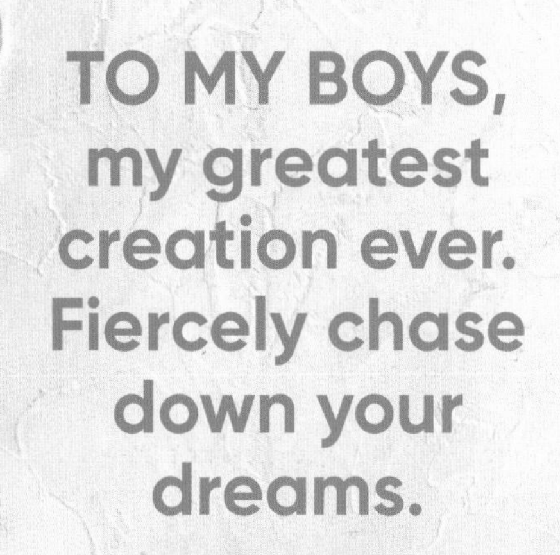

TO MY BOYS,
my greatest
creation ever.
Fiercely chase
down your
dreams.

Contents

Chapter 6

Soups and Green Salads 189

Chapter 7

Side Dishes 211

Chapter 8

Sauces and Seasonings 249

Chapter 9

Desserts 271

Foreword

I'd like to think I know Autumn pretty well. She's a Whole30 HQ team member, a Whole30 Certified Coach, a successful recipe developer and blogger, and a wife and mother of five. I've watched her blog and recipe channel grow, I've promoted her to her current role as the Whole30 Coaching Manager, and I eagerly follow her family's backpacking and hiking adventures on Instagram. Autumn seems to accomplish more in a week than many people do in a month, and yet I never ask myself, "How does she do it?"

Sounds weird, right? For years now, I've watched her gracefully toggle between work, family, and her passion for cooking and the outdoors, achieving success in both her career and personal pursuits in tandem. It's not that I'm unimpressed—I'm *tremendously* impressed and personally motivated by everything Autumn does.

The reason I don't need to ask, "How does she do it?" is because she is deeply committed to showing us in a radically authentic, accessible, relatable way *exactly* how she does it. It's what I love the most about her and why I follow all her content and offerings with devotion. She's real and honest and shows us real-life stuff, not just carefully-curated-Instagram-worthy stuff. And that's exactly why I never need to ask and I am always inspired.

That day she had to FaceTime from our team offsite because her son couldn't find his volleyball jersey? She shared that in a gripping Instagram saga. (After an hour on the phone, he still couldn't find it—but she found it within minutes once she got home, hashtag momlife.) The morning her pool exploded and she had to navigate a drenched backyard around her Zoom calls? She shared pictures with the eye roll emoji. The day she realized her kid's carpool situation had changed and she had to drive four hours round trip to grab him from his prestigious music camp? Every parent everywhere could relate to her frustration but also pride but also annoyance but also excitement to spend two whole hours *all by herself*, followed by two whole hours of quality time with her kid.

I KNOW how Autumn does it because she generously shares so much of her life with her team and community. She does it one day at a time, as best as she can, imperfectly, and with a great sense of humor. Autumn is all of us if all of us could bake like an angel and feed a family of seven cookbook-worthy meals on a tight budget. It's why I trust her and why you should trust her, too, as you're working hard to eat healthier and bring your family along on the journey.

Maybe, like me, you can't bake like an angel. (That's an understatement.) Maybe you're new to prepping and cooking whole, real food for your family and not sure how you'll find the time. Perhaps you're also on a tight budget, wondering how you can balance your finances with your desire to make healthy, satisfying, delicious meals. Wherever you're coming from, you're in the right place—because Autumn was there, too. Not that long ago, Autumn was a self-described sugar addict, uncertain about how to cook and eat healthy and do it all within her family's financial capacity and busy schedule. But she *has* done it, and now through this Whole30-endorsed book, she's showing you how you can, too, in a way that feels accessible and relatable.

Whole Food for Your Family is full of delicious, hearty recipes using ingredients from your regular neighborhood grocery store, tried and tested in Autumn's own kitchen, approved by the pickiest critics (her kids). She's included her best tips for getting started on your Whole30 or healthy eating journey, how to maximize your time in the kitchen and make meal prep efficient, and exactly how she sticks to her budget while feeding five hungry boys. Most of all, she'll show you that eating healthy, whether you're cooking for one or seven, really can be easy, rewarding, and refreshingly delicious.

This book is full of Autumn's most valuable learnings, highest-rated family recipes, and the kind of patient, sincere, humorous encouragement she is known for. Whether you're just starting your family's healthy-eating journey or looking to solidify your existing healthy habits, you're in the best possible hands. And when your friends, family, and coworkers start asking you, "Wow—how do you do it?" you can hand them this book with a smile. (Just make sure you get it back.)

Best in health,

Melissa

Melissa Urban
Whole30 Co-Founder and CEO

Prologue

I see you.

I see those of you who are:

- Wondering if you can eat nourishing foods on a budget
- Not sure if you have time to cook
- Navigating feeding picky eaters and tired of making separate meals
- Intimidated by changing the way your family eats
- Struggling to have energy to cook after a long day of work
- Trying to keep up with the demands of feeding a (large) family
- Wanting to eat wholesome food that is *actually* delicious
- Making dinner with a toddler hanging on your leg and a baby in your arms
- Craving simple, unfussy recipes
- Looking for family-friendly options

This book is for you. I hope it empowers you in the kitchen and blesses your family.

Introduction

My Whole30 Experience: A Family Story

I was terrified to change the way my family ate.

Thanks to several rounds of Whole30 and lots of Food Freedom work, I had completely changed my own relationship with food, including taming a fierce sugar dragon. But the thought of extending those changes to my family—especially my large family of five growing boys, aka "walking stomachs"—sounded overwhelming.

I tried to feed my boys well: the crackers were whole grain; we enjoyed lots of fruit; and we tried to avoid having soda and chips on the regular. But my kids didn't like much protein, like chicken or beef, or most veggies, so they mostly ate cereal and snacks, and we leaned more heavily on processed foods and five-dollar pizzas than I wanted to admit.

They were also embarrassingly picky: didn't want to take them to a church potluck because they would come out of the line with only a plate of shredded cheese and a roll kind of picky. True story. I was that kid growing up—the picky kid who did not think I could eat foods outside of my small list of favorites. I didn't learn to like vegetables until I was twenty-one. The only veggies I ate growing up were peas, potatoes, and corn. So I could empathize with my boys—I knew what picky felt like. I also thought that I turned out OK, wouldn't they?

So what changed? What finally pushed me to change the way I eat and eventually bring my family on board? To answer that question, we have to start at the beginning.

My Struggles with Sugar

Growing up in Houston, Texas, I didn't think much about my relationship with food. I was a tall dancer who loved desserts. I felt healthy enough eating the foods that fell within my picky palate, and I never thought much of it.

When I earned a degree in exercise physiology from Brigham Young University, health became not just a passion of mine but my profession. During my last two years of college, I led the BYU Employee Wellness Program and loved running programs and challenges to help people live healthier. I had a naïve understanding of health then and believed it was as simple as "move more, eat less."

I set my career aside after graduation. I married at nineteen and started having kids when I was twenty-one years old. I was so pregnant during graduation that I literally waddled across the stage to get my diploma and had my first boy a week later. My boys are like stair steps—we had one every two years for ten years. Yes, we wanted a large family (we both come from one); yes, they came one at a time; and no, we are not still trying for a girl!

A few children in, the stress of having three kids under five was wearing on me. I turned more and more to sweets as a crutch. It seemed like a harmless way to soothe myself, and I would joke about having a "sweet tooth." Before too long, I went from eating dessert after dinner to dessert with lunch and dinner and then finally to the point where I would rather eat sweets all day than real food. I rationalized that if it was just a matter of "calories in, calories out," then what did it matter if most of the calories were from dessert?

The first time I stared that sugar dragon in the eyes and finally acknowledged this wasn't healthy, I called my best friend sobbing because I felt so out of control. I described my sugar obsession as a "monkey on my back"—the desire to eat sweets was always there, pestering me, demanding my attention all day long.

It didn't feel right that food should take so much of my energy. I was ashamed to admit it out loud. Putting it into words was hard; it was so much easier to pretend the problem didn't exist.

My First Whole30—Which I Didn't Finish

My battle with sugar continued through several moves and two more kids. Then, in 2013, my husband was having some health challenges, and his naturopath suggested he try the Whole30. The Whole30 is a reset that can help change your health, habits, and relationship with food as well as identify foods that may not be working for your body. It does so by eliminating commonly problematic food groups for 30 days to reset the body. Then you add those foods one at a time (called *reintroduction*) to see what worked best for you—and what didn't. My exact reaction was, "This is too extreme," and I tossed the paperwork aside.

By this time, I was a certified personal trainer, gym manager, and aerobics instructor, and I believed the main path to health was exercise. I worked out a lot, was strong, and believed I was healthy. But my nagging sugar dragon was always lurking in the background. I would hide treats in my baby's bedroom, thinking I would have to be crazy to go in there when he was sleeping and risk waking him. It didn't work. I would find myself digging through the closet to get my hidden stash at all hours.

I tried moderation—that's what we taught at my gym and in my college classes: All things in "moderation." I set limits—*I am only going to eat two treats a week*. I shared my goals with other people to help hold myself accountable. But moderation felt so . . . impossible. The foods I wanted had no brakes, and I would fall short of my goals again and again. I felt like such a hypocrite to be so strong in the gym and such a mess around food.

Ultimately, I was exhausted by my food struggles. Out of desperation, I found that Whole30 handout. It was simple enough, with a clear list of foods to eat and not eat. I dove in without much further thought, preparation, or research. For 30 days, I just wouldn't eat the food not allowed. I didn't tell anyone I was doing it, so I wouldn't look like a failure if it didn't work out. I didn't last longer than day 10 before nose-diving back into my treats. I felt so guilty that I couldn't even go without sweets for 30 days. But the experience fired up something in me.

A few months later, I did another Whole30, but this time I had done some research online. I read *It Starts with Food*, a book that opened my eyes to the complex relationship we have with food. It talked about why some foods are nearly impossible to eat in moderation, or "foods with no brakes." It explained that my problem wasn't that I lacked willpower or that I was lazy. It was that these foods were full of stimulating, highly processed ingredients designed to make you want more. To this day, *It Starts with Food* is one of my favorite nutrition books, and I highly recommend it if you want to learn the basic science of food. After reading it that first time, things started to click.

Reintroduction—Where the Real Magic Happens

I wish I could tell you it was smooth sailing from there, but it wasn't. About a month after my first successful Whole30, I was pretty much right back to where I started, but now I was carrying extra guilt for returning to my unhealthy habits.

Then I realized I had missed a key component of Whole30—the reintroduction. Reintroduction is the systematic process where you add back the foods you take out during a Whole30: grains, gluten, dairy, alcohol, legumes, and sweeteners. Reintroduction matters because it shows you which foods might be connected to negative reactions in your body.

For example, thanks to reintroduction, I learned that dairy and sugar contribute to my adult acne. I struggled with acne from ages thirteen to thirty-three. I had asked my dermatologist if it could be affected by my diet, but she promptly dismissed the idea and put me on some harsh topical creams and medicine. But during Whole30, my skin was *fantastic*. Through reintroduction, I was able to connect that to the absence of dairy and white sugar. By removing those from my regular diet, I was able to get off the strong acne meds and creams, which felt like a miracle after decades of skin struggles. Even my dermatologist asked me what I was doing when she saw how good my skin looked. I told her my discovery, and she looked at me and said, "No, that can't be it." My experience disagrees.

I was also a "chronic napper" and behind-my-eyes tired, even after sleeping seven-ish hours most nights. I would fall asleep midsentence while reading books to my sons, until my oldest elbowed me to wake up and read. Every parent is tired, so I assumed this was just life, until I tried Whole30 and experienced constant energy—no 2:00 p.m. slump! I realized that gluten makes me tired and that fatigue is compounded by the constant blood sugar spikes that come from eating sweets. Once I removed gluten and processed sugar from my daily diet, I noticed an incredible difference in my energy. Now napping is the rare exception, not the norm.

Whole30 also improved and leveled my moods. I used to call 5:00 p.m. the "armpit of the day." I was a tired mom trying to get dinner ready with young kids underfoot. More often than I would like to admit, I was grouchy and would lose my temper. I wanted to do better, and I had goals to be positive and calm, but I struggled. It sounds simplistic, but taking gluten and refined sugar out of my diet did a 180 on my mood. I felt in charge of my emotions: the moodiness and snappiness didn't have control over me anymore. It didn't eliminate the bad days, but it made my emotions more stable, and I felt like I could respond to the challenges of motherhood with more resilience. I was less on edge.

I thought things like acne, fatigue, and moodiness were just part of life, not things I could change and definitely not through food. I've heard it from so many clients, and I know it sounds like a bad infomercial, but what I learned from Whole30 truly helped me become my best self. It's hugely empowering to learn the strong connection between what you eat and how you feel and look. The goal isn't to eat Whole30 for the rest of your life. It's to discover how foods work with your body and make educated choices about what foods work best in your life.

My Whole30 was so life-changing that I was inspired to guide other people through the experience. We held some group Whole30 challenges at my local gym and place of work, The Training Zone. I loved seeing that lightbulb go off for people. One of my favorites was Nancy, a client who was seventy-six years old and never thought she could feel so young and spry.

As soon as Whole30 announced there was going to be a coaching certification, I started working on my application. In October 2017, I became one of the first Whole30 Certified Coaches and started working for Whole30 in February 2018.

My Food-Freedom Work

Life and progress aren't linear, and neither was my relationship with sugar. I had more lows before it got better long term, even after several successful Whole30s and reintroduction. I would make a batch of brownies or cookies, and my boys would wonder where all the extras went. I would lie to my husband, saying I needed to run to a friend's house, only to head to the corner market, buy chocolate Ding Dongs or donuts and milk, eat them in the car, throw away the evidence, and then return home, swearing to myself that I wouldn't do it again. There were a lot of tears and shame. It felt heavy and impossible. Looking back, I wish I had gone to an eating disorder counselor, but I had no idea such a thing existed.

In 2016, Whole30 co-founder Melissa Urban published *Food Freedom Forever*. I remember sitting on my couch reading it and just saying, "YES! Yes!" I felt so seen and not alone. I loved the tangible tips and strategies it shared and leaped into them with both feet.

I started tracking my triggers—situations that were driving me to binge on sugar. I printed a calendar, titled it "Mommy's Sugar Challenge," and put it on the fridge. We were no strangers to sticker reward charts in our house, and I was not above using tried-and-true parenting techniques on myself. I put a sticker on days I felt in control of my relationship with food and took notes on days I wasn't. I started to see patterns and triggers, which I could then deal with head-on instead of with sugar.

For example, Sunday evenings were hard for me. I realized that when my family was relaxing after church and I was in the kitchen cooking a big Sunday dinner, I felt angry and resentful that I couldn't relax, too, and that no one was helping. That anger and stress led to emotional eating. After seeing the pattern, I talked to my husband, who, it turns out, didn't care if we ate simple Sunday meals so I could relax, too. Dealing with the root of the problem, the trigger, was so much more effective than soothing with food.

Baking was also triggering for me. I adore baking; it's so wonderfully sensory. I was known for my baked goods and was regularly asked to bring them to social gatherings. But baking often ended up with me nose-diving into a bowl of cookie dough. So for about six months, I didn't bake. You need me to bring a treat to a church potluck? Sure thing, but it will be store-bought. My friend LeeAnna, who has POTS, an autoimmune disorder, compared it to someone who has a broken bone and wants to go running. If you have a broken leg, running is a terrible idea until you're fully healed. Running isn't bad in and of itself, but if you run on a broken bone, you don't give yourself the opportunity to heal. I needed a break from baking. Baking wasn't bad in and of itself, but it was really triggering for me, and I needed a break to heal. Now I bake often and love it without being triggered by it.

I also continued to build my plate the way Whole30 taught me—FULL of veggies, one or two palm-sized servings of protein, and healthy fat. Eating nutrient-dense food really helped the cravings diminish, especially when I abandoned my fat-phobia from the nineties and included healthy fat on my plate at every meal. Many of my clients have said eating more healthy fats was a game-changer for them when it came to eliminating their cravings and boosting their energy and moods. (Again, if you want to take a deeper dive into the science behind this way of eating, I recommend reading *It Starts with Food*.)

I wish everyone who does a Whole30 would put as much work into their food freedom as they do their Whole30. Doing so was a key piece in healing my relationship with food.

Why Our Family Transitioned to a Paleo-ish Diet

So back to my initial question: What inspired me to bring my whole family on board?

By 2017, I had done several successful rounds of Whole30 and guided dozens of clients through it as well. I was incredibly empowered in my relationship with food. The more I leaned into these dietary changes, the more I realized that my boys deserved these benefits as well. But every time this thought bubbled up, I would silence the idea. There were too many reasons against changing our family's diet: it was too intimidating, too expensive, too much.

In the end, I didn't have to convince my family to change the way they ate; I was leading and inspiring them by example. My boys noticed the change in my eating habits and were curious. They asked why their dad, Matt, and I were no longer eating gluten, dairy, or refined sugar. I enthusiastically told them the answer and how positive these changes had been for me. I wasn't prepared for the next question: "Well, when can we try it?"

I thought about taking baby steps, maybe taking out just dairy or gluten. After overthinking it, I eventually decided to lean on something familiar: What if we did a 30-day family experiment? I told the boys that we would take out dairy, gluten, and refined sugar for 30 days and see what happened. If it was too hard or didn't produce significant changes, we would be done.

You're probably thinking that the 30-day time limit was to talk them into it, but really it was to talk *me* into it.

I realized that there would be no perfect time to make this change. I am a woman of action, so I just went for it during one of the most dynamic months of the year for us, July. We play hard in the summer, and we were traveling half of July 2017. The good thing about traveling? It's already a new and different situation.

We had a family meeting, and I told them about our plan. I explained why we were going to change our eating habits, sharing the positive results Matt and I had experienced, and answering any questions. Together, we made a plan of what we could still eat and looked through cookbooks together. I'm not going to lie; it was a little difficult because there weren't a lot of family-friendly Paleo/Whole30 cookbooks then, so I truly hope *this* cookbook can be a resource for you!

Day 30 came and went without much notice. My kids had found a new rhythm and weren't chomping at the bit to stop. But I decided eventually, around day 40, to take inventory on this family experiment. I pulled each boy aside privately and asked for their honest feedback on how it all went. Their responses blew me away:

- I'm a lot less hungry all the time.
- I get fewer stomachaches.
- My brother is less moody.*
- I can control myself (said the less-moody brother from the above comment).
- I'm happier and my brothers are kinder.
- I sleep better.
- I like all the cool new foods.
- My skin looks so good (said my thirteen-year-old, whose acne cleared up).

---

*One of my boys was a spirited kiddo, prone to lots of over-the-top emotions and fits. It was challenging to parent, and it affected our family dynamic. This lifestyle has dramatically changed that for the better, which was a game-changer for me.

Surprisingly, not one of them asked to go back to our old way of eating. Every once in a while, the kids will see something we used to eat and mention how they kind of miss it. I will say, "Yeah, I miss some foods, too. But the way they make me feel is not worth it." My kids will usually nod and agree. By the time this book comes out, it will have been five years since we made this shift.

Change can become your new normal, too.

How to Use This Book

Wherever you're starting on your Whole30 or health journey, this book is for you.

All the recipes in this book are gluten-free and dairy-free. That's just how my family eats. Almost all of them are Paleo as well, and most are Whole30-compatible. This book is excellent if you're doing a Whole30, and it includes some great food freedom options (hello, dessert chapter!) to help make eating whole foods a sustainable lifestyle after the 30 days.

My recipes are kid-friendly but not just for kids. I love recipes that aren't fussy. This collection is filled with staples that are simple and easy to make, recipes that fit in your daily life, with lots of modifications and options to make them accessible.

You don't need a lot of fancy equipment to cook from this book (see Pantry and Kitchen Essentials on page 25). That said, I love my air fryer, so there are many recipes that can be made in the oven but include an air fryer option.

As a mom, I find myself thinking about *meals* more than just recipes, so I add pairing recommendations (Make It a Meal) for some recipes and suggest sides that complement different mains so you can easily build a complete meal.

Since your freezer can be your best friend when it comes to feeding a family this way (see How Do You Feed All Those Boys? on page 13), I also note when meals are freezer friendly, as well as nut-free, egg-free, or Whole30-compatible. (A grayed out icon means the recipe can be adapted for your dietary needs or cooking preferences.) →

From energizing breakfasts to satisfying mains, comforting desserts, and even easy whole foods lunches, my hope was to make this way of eating easy and delicious for every meal.

I hope this cookbook will be the empowering resource I wanted when my family started this journey.

I see you, and you can do this.

Look for these icons to tell you when something is **Whole30-compatible** WHOLE 30, **nut-free**, **egg-free**, **freezer-friendly**, can be prepared in **30 minutes** 30, and can be made in the **air fryer**.

Tips for Dealing with Picky Eaters

Oh, the things my husband and I have tried in an effort to get our kids to eat their meals. We have tried the "eat as many bites as you are old" trick. We have made them take at least X number of "thank-you" bites to make sure they at least tried it. We have forbidden any sweets or snacks after dinner unless they have eaten a certain amount of the main meal. We have made them finish the small amounts they put on their plates. And we have bribed them with various desserts if they have eaten however many bites.

And if they didn't eat all their bites? We would make them stay at the table until they did. Once my second son literally, I kid you not, chewed a piece of chicken for over thirty minutes. I had no idea that was possible! We've had several instances of children throwing up after they ate their forced bites. My fourth son is convinced he is "allergic" to Brussels sprouts after one especially dramatic incident.

We've tried it all, and yet none of it gave my kids a good relationship with food, and every technique made dinner a *battle*. "How many bites do I have to have?" "Have I eaten enough to get dessert?" It was exhausting and an ongoing power struggle, and I can't recommend any of it.

But fear not. We did learn a few helpful tips over the years. Here are some tried-and-true techniques that *have* worked to help our picky eaters (Note: These tips are not intended as medical advice and may not be appropriate for children with sensory or other feeding issues or diagnoses.):

1. Division of Responsibility—Control Only What You Actually Can Control

In college, our nutrition professor taught us the work of Ellyn Satter, and I keep coming back to it. I especially loved her teachings on the "division of responsibility" at a meal. As parents, our job is to dictate *what*, *where*, and *when* to feed. The child's job is to choose *how much to eat* or *whether to eat* from what the parents offer.

At first, I was intimidated to try it. What if they didn't eat anything? When I finally tried Satter's approach, her method took the pressure off me for things I couldn't really control—how much my kids ate—and has worked really well for us.

2. Make Sure Your Kids Are Coming to Meals Hungry

My children are school age and get home by 3:00 p.m. Snacks are only available until 3:30 p.m., and then I cut off the grazing before dinner. The kitchen is generally *closed* between snack and dinner. Yes, that might sound daunting, but like anything with parenting, if you are consistent on the rules, kids adjust. Consistently enforce it for a week or two, and you might be surprised!

3. Keep Offering Foods and Be Consistent

At dinner, all foods are passed around, and I encourage my kids to try it without bribes or forcing it. It can take up to fifteen to thirty exposures to a food before a child will try it. I bite my tongue and do not reprimand my child if their plate is sparsely filled one night. (Trust me, this is hard sometimes!) Whether my kids choose to try something new, there is no battle of wills or forced bites anymore. That's *their* job at the dinner table. When dinner is done, so is eating for the night . . . period. There will be another meal waiting for them at breakfast; they will survive and learn. Again, consistency is key! Consistency is one of the *hardest* things to do as a parent, but one of the most crucial skills to master to make effective changes.

4. Involve Your Kids in the Process

My kids regularly help in the kitchen and occasionally with meal planning. This encourages them to connect with the food. When it's *their* creation and choice, they feel more empowered and are more likely to eat the finished product. I don't always have the patience for this, particularly when dinner needs to get on the table quickly, but I try to do it at least a few times a week, especially during the summer.

5. Don't Empower Their Pickiness

For years, I thought I was making my life easier by having "kid" options at dinner. If I made something like soup, an "adult" food that I didn't think my kids would like, I would also make grilled cheeses or quesadillas. I did so more often than I would like to admit. Because I was a picky eater, I would feel guilty serving food I "knew" my kids wouldn't like.

I did this to avoid a battle and to keep my kids from getting malnourished. But this just empowered their pickiness. It gave them permission to not try new things because the familiar favorites were always available. I was essentially giving them a free pass from branching out and was shooting myself in the foot.

And what do you know, now my boys all like soup.

How Do You Feed All Those Boys?

I have a confession: I don't like bulk meal prepping. You know, where you take four-ish hours and prep most of your meals for the week all at once. I have done it, but it has always left me feeling grumpy. The only days of the week when I had that kind of time were Saturday and Sunday, and giving up half a weekend day to meal prepping left me feeling frustrated. I'd rather spend my weekends making memories with my family or relaxing and recharging for the week to come.

There are a lot of reasons people don't like to meal prep:

- We don't know what we will be in the mood for later in the week.
- Getting organized can be overwhelming.
- If we get tired of the food we prepped, the food gets wasted.
- We don't always like the taste of leftovers.

That said, as a Whole30 Coach who has helped more than a thousand clients, I can tell you hands-down that having healthy food options prepped and ready to grab is game-changing. It's so much easier to stay committed to your nutrition goals when the food is already prepped.

So here are my painless tips for meal prepping without giving up your precious weekend time.

Make Something Extra

I realized I didn't have to have all my meals for the week cooked and ready on Sunday; I just always had to have options available for upcoming meals. So I started *Make Something Extra*—every time I cook, I make more than I know we're going to eat at that meal. The idea is to break the sometimes overwhelming job of meal prepping into manageable chunks throughout the week instead of having that big weekend marathon.

I ask myself two questions:

1. What do I have on hand and need to use up? This helps prevent food waste and is budget-friendly. (The average person throws away fifty dollars a month in food waste!)
2. What do I need more of? This doesn't have to be a whole meal. Maybe you need to pull together a great sauce, some roasted veggies, or grilled meat. Do you have anything for breakfast the next day? If not, put together a breakfast dish that you can reheat and eat for the next few days.

Meal prepping in these increments also allows for a little more flexibility if you've got a sudden craving for something or an idea for a new dish, because you are doing it several times throughout the week instead of seven days in advance.

Maximize Time in the Kitchen

When I'm cooking, I aim to maximize my time already spent in the kitchen by making an additional item or dish while cooking the original meal. You're already cooking, so instead of scrolling through your phone while something simmers or the oven preheats, prep something for tomorrow night's dinner or lunch. A casual survey of my community said that they cook six to eleven times per week on average. That's six to eleven *extra* sides, sauces, or entrées that could be prepped for the week with minimal extra time spent.

You're Going to Double Batch That . . . Right?

If you're making a recipe that you know you love, why not double it? Doubling a dish is a very easy way to make something extra. You might think, *But Autumn, I will get sick of eating this every day for the next week*. No, no, friend; it's time to embrace the freezer! My mom froze eeeverything. So double batch, eat it for a few days, and when you are no longer enjoying it, put the rest in the freezer (labeled with the date and name, so you can identify it later). In three to four weeks, you will be so grateful to be able to pull it out and reheat it on a busy night! Your future self will thank you. *Many of my recipes are freezer-friendly—look for the* **freezer icon** *at the top of the recipe.*

Don't Like the Taste of Leftovers?

This is where the air fryer can really shine. Roasted veggies get soggy in the fridge, but they can easily "recrisp" in the air fryer. Air fryers can also reheat meat without drying it out, as the oil circulates in the air.

How Does Your Family Deal with Eating Healthy *Outside of* the Home?

I get asked this a lot, and my answer surprises people. I have focused on healthy eating *inside* our home. I control what's coming into our house. As the adult with the car and the wallet, that's both within my control and something I feel I owe to my kids to take responsibility for.

But I have not tried to control the outside social situations. If someone brings cupcakes to school for a birthday, it's my kids' choice whether they have one. If they are at a sleepover and offered pizza, the choice is theirs.

For me, this comes down to picking my battles. If I feed them wholesome meals at home, I know the rare or occasional treat out won't be significantly detrimental to their progress or health. I also keep a supply of Paleo treats at home. If they choose to pass on a treat at school or elsewhere, they know they can have a gluten-free, dairy-free treat when they get home. I have been shocked by how often my kids will do this—pass on the dessert with gluten/dairy/refined sugar in it and wait for the healthier option at home. Why? Because they have had enough personal experiences with how these foods make them feel to intrinsically not want to eat them. That's something that no rules would enforce; they had to learn it for themselves.

Could I control those situations? Sure, or at least I could try. But I don't want to restrict to the point that they are driven to bingeing or having a constant power struggle. Plus, there is no way I can control every situation. They are not with me 24/7. I believe in teaching them the principles and then letting them govern themselves. My oldest stays 100 percent compliant to the Paleo lifestyle by choice. One of my others would definitely eat a donut if you handed it to him. But at least I am empowering their future with education, tools, and the reality of how "normal" and delicious whole-food eating can be.

What about Extended Family?

Another issue that comes up when you shift your family's food habits is the question of extended family. I get it. This can be tricky.

Our family has been supportive, but I understand how difficult it would be if they weren't. If you are in that position, I highly encourage you to read *Food Freedom Forever*'s Chapter 11, which focuses on how to talk to others and offers solutions and strategies to navigate tricky family and social situations. I love that it begins with a reminder that "Food isn't just food. In our relationships, food is love, acceptance, bonding and comfort."

Eating Well on a Budget

Often, Whole30 and whole-food eating get a bad rap for being too expensive or requiring fancy ingredients or pricey convenience products. This is simply not the case. You can eat healthy on a budget!* And you don't need specialty grocery stores, either. Case in point: we shop almost exclusively at Walmart and Winco (the US West Coast version of Aldi).

Why do I care about eating healthy on a budget? My husband and I started our family during our college years. As "starving students," we were grateful for programs like WIC and food stamps to help get us through. Once my husband got his first "real" job, moving cross-country to Florida devoured our savings, and money did not stretch as far as we thought it would. We were broke. We made just enough to not qualify for food stamps the way we did in college but not enough to be comfortable. Money was painfully tight. I'm talking turning off the AC during a Florida summer to save money, owning one car, and walking most places pushing a double stroller to save on gas. I'm not saying my hard is harder than your hard; only that I know that feeling when money is constantly a weight on your back as you struggle to cover the needs, no less the wants.

*It would be presumptuous to say that everyone can afford to eat healthy. That does not acknowledge those who can barely put food of any kind on the table or live in a food desert. Eating a particular way (Paleo, Whole30, Keto, etc.) is a privilege, and I want to acknowledge that. While I hope that my budget-friendly recipes and tips make healthy eating more approachable, I know that it still is not accessible to all.

That's not our life now, but we have five boys to feed and who we'd eventually like to send to college, so I'm still mindful of how much we spend on our weekly groceries. Here are some tips to eating well on a budget:

Tip #1: Stick to Your List

My first tip is intuitive to some but worth mentioning: you can't afford *not* to meal plan. Literally. Every time you walk into a store, you open up the potential to overspend. When you go to a store without a meal plan and specific list, you will pick up items you didn't actually need. Also, without a specific meal plan and a list, there's a strong chance that you won't get all the things you actually did need this week, which means you'll spend more gas going back to the store, where you risk buying more things that you don't need or you'll spend more on staples out of convenience. (Here's looking at you, corner market.) Straight from the expert of saving himself, Dave Ramsey: "A list can make or break a budget." Meal plan, shop with a list, and stick to that list!

How do I meal plan? I picked a day of the week that works for my schedule to regularly meal plan, which for me is Saturday. I sit down with a piece of paper and fold it in half to divide it into two columns. On one side, I list the meals we are going to be eating for the week; on the other side, I list the ingredients needed for those meals, usually divided by the grocery store I know from experience will have the best price on each item. I also try to list the items on my shopping list by area of the store so as to make my grocery trips more efficient. I typically shop at two or three different stores each week to get the best deals.

Each week, I pick out about five dinner recipes, plus a few breakfast and lunch items. This will be enough for a week of meals, as some nights are just leftovers or something on the fly. I don't assign the meals to a specific day, as I prefer the flexibility to decide that throughout the week.

I will normally snag one or two of the kids to help me pick recipes because they are more likely to eat the meals they picked. Kids are naturally drawn to photos, so they like to sit down and flip through cookbooks with me and point out the things that look good. Of course, sometimes when I ask them what I should make for the upcoming week, they just say, "Hot dogs." To try to build our family food vocabulary, at least one meal each meal planning session is a new recipe to try. Also, to keep up with the demands of a large family, I double most meals and freeze any extras or serve the leftovers for lunch the next day.

Tip #2: Waste Not, Want Not

Your food is basically edible cash. You spent hard-earned money on those groceries. Don't let it go into the trash can! The average American throws out $640 worth of food a year. That's roughly $50 a month tossed right in the trash. Having a meal plan, making a list, and sticking to it prevent that waste. On weekends, I use up all the leftovers or cook about-to-spoil veggies. Not gonna eat something right away? Freeze it! Most cooked foods can last months in the freezer. (Look for the freezer-friendly **freezer icon** on the recipes in this book.)

Shop your own pantry and refrigerator before you go to the store. After I pick my meals for the week and make my grocery list, I take the list to the pantry and fridge and cross off the items I already have. I once bought Dijon mustard every other week for eight weeks because I kept forgetting that I already had it. Shopping my pantry would have prevented that!

Tip #3: Make It Yourself!

Premade products are convenient, but you pay for that convenience! If that's not an option for you, then it's time to learn how to make it yourself. This is also a necessity if you don't have easy access to Whole30-compatible items like mayo, dressings, and seasonings.

Just like learning how to drive a car, cooking can take a lot of focus at first, but eventually that 20-minute mayo becomes 2-minute mayo you can make while pulling together dinner and helping the eight-year-old with his math homework. Trust me! I have lots of awesome staples in this book from delicious, easy sauces and spreads to basics like ghee and nut butter (see Sauces and Seasonings starting on page 249).

Tip #4: Make Do or Do Without

Growing up, my mom always loved the saying, "Use it up, wear it out, make do, or do without!" We already talked about "using up" your food by shopping with a list and sticking to a meal plan, then incorporating leftovers into your weekly meal plan to make sure you're not wasting food. "Make do or do without" means knowing what foods you can swap out and when you can leave something out altogether. For example, when making the homemade chicken apple sausage recipe in my Breakfast Salad (page 51), I sometimes buy ground turkey instead of ground chicken because it can be up to $1.50 per pound less. Ground chicken and turkey are very interchangeable—make do with whichever one is cheaper or on sale! Or in my homemade Whole30 BBQ Sauce recipe (page 256), coconut aminos can be expensive or hard to source, but the recipe also works without that ingredient, so you can "do without" without sacrificing on taste.

One of my favorite budget swaps is using dried herbs in place of fresh. Fresh herbs almost always taste better . . . but they can get pricey, and they never last long. Did you know you can usually swap dried herbs with fresh? Just use one-third the amount! If a recipe calls for 3 tablespoons of chopped fresh basil, you can use 1 tablespoon of dried basil instead. Dried herbs last a lot longer than fresh, too, so there's less chance of them spoiling and ending up in the trash. I use a lot of dried spices in this book because they are more affordable and they have such a long shelf life. I worked hard in this cookbook to include only essential ingredients and to give you as many modifications as I could, both for dietary and budget needs.

Tip #5: Let Good Enough Be Good Enough

This last tip is based on a common Whole30 catch phrase: "Let good enough be good enough." Now, if you are on a Whole30, there are some pretty strict rules—no consuming grains, dairy, legumes, sugar, alcohol; making comparable baked goods; or weighing yourself. Period. I'm not talking about being flexible on any of those. What I'm talking about is not feeling like you have to purchase organic or grass-fed everything to be successful at a Whole30 or healthy eating, because you don't. Are organic veggies and responsibly raised meat sources ideal? Absolutely! But if you are truly on a budget, you may barely (if at all) afford regular steak, no less grass-fed.

To be honest, my family of seven does not eat grass-fed meat or exclusively organic produce. *Gasp!* There, I said it. Our food budget is already stretched thin to make whole-food eating for seven work. I'd love to buy only organic and grass-fed, but it just isn't happening. My family has still seen incredible benefits from whole-food and Whole30 eating without it.

In other words, don't miss the forest for the trees; buy the best quality you can afford, and let good enough be good enough! A home-cooked meal is still an awesome success regardless of whether the meat is grass-fed.

SEEDS
COCOA
baking
POWDER
nutritional
YEAST
table
SALT
maple
SUGAR
coconut
FLOUR
Potato
STARCH
Cassava
FLOUR
Tapioca
FLOUR
Almond
FLOUR
coconut
SUGAR

Pantry and Kitchen Essentials

I try to make my recipes as flexible and as approachable as possible, by using ingredients you can buy at most grocery stores. There are a few ingredients that are tougher to source but are used frequently and are worth tracking down.

Flours

- **ALMOND FLOUR:** I prefer super-fine almond flour (I buy Blue Diamond brand, which I find at Sam's Club). If it's not super-fine, it will still work, but it will result in a grittier texture in baked goods. Almond flour is awesome to use instead of bread crumbs in breading and helps give gluten-free baked goods some bulk and volume. If you can't eat nuts, I provided nut-free options for most recipes, which often call for cassava flour (see page 26).
- **TAPIOCA, ARROWROOT, OR POTATO FLOUR OR STARCH:** These are often interchangeable. They are great as thickeners, though I usually prefer arrowroot and potato starch for thickeners, as tapioca flour/starch will thicken a sauce but leave it a bit tacky. Tapioca is my preferred starch for baking and breading.

- **COCONUT FLOUR:** Coconut flour is unique in its ability to thicken a baked good. It's incredibly absorbent and will soak up moisture. Recipes that use coconut flour will usually tell you to set the batter aside and wait 5 minutes, as this allows the flour to soak up the moisture and get to the right consistency.
- **CASSAVA FLOUR:** Cassava flour is made from yucca root and is the closest a grain-free flour can get to traditional white flour. It's definitely not a 1:1 ratio for white flour; it's more like ¾ cup cassava flour is equal to 1 cup white flour. It is also my recommended flour for those who want to eat grain-free but are avoiding nuts. Most of my nut-free baked goods use cassava flour.

Sugars

- **COCONUT SUGAR:** The primary granulated sweetener used in Paleo baking, coconut sugar is made using sap from the flower buds of a coconut tree that is heated and dried to form sugar granules. It's brown in color and has a rich flavor similar to brown sugar.
- **MAPLE SUGAR:** This also comes from the sap of a tree and is basically a granulated version of maple syrup. Though it does have a slight maple flavor, its granules are smaller, so it behaves more like white sugar than coconut sugar. Coconut sugar and maple sugar are interchangeable, but maple sugar tends to work better in baked goods.

READ YOUR LABELS

On a Whole30? Just a reminder that you need to double-check any store-bought, packaged items to make sure they are Whole30-compatible. For example, store-bought ketchups or bacon often have added sugar and are not Whole30-compatible. If you are on a Whole30 or want to adhere to the Whole30 principles as much as possible, be sure to read labels when sourcing some ingredients used in this book such as ketchup, bacon, and frozen hash browns; as well as canned goods such as diced tomatoes, tomato sauce, or coconut cream; deli meats (including pepperoni); pickles; coconut aminos; and dairy-free cheeses (allowed with caution on Whole30 if ingredients are compatible).

Other Pantry Items

- **CANNED COCONUT MILK:** I love coconut milk for its thick, almost cream-like consistency. When I call for coconut milk, I am referring to canned, full-fat, unsweetened coconut milk. My preferred brand is Thai Kitchen because of its more subtle coconut flavor and thick texture.
- **CANNED COCONUT CREAM:** I use this often in place of heavy cream or sour cream. It has a higher fat content than coconut milk, so it's thicker. To keep the mixture thick, in most of my recipes, I use only the solid part of the can. The cream only separates out when chilled, so I usually just store my canned coconut cream in the fridge. I set aside the remaining milky liquid to use in smoothies. I prefer Thai Kitchen canned coconut cream that I buy at Walmart. (Yes, the solid cream that rises to the top of a chilled can of coconut milk is also coconut cream, but you will need 2 or 3 cans of that to equal 1 can of coconut cream, and it isn't as thick due to a lower fat content.)
- **GHEE:** I had never heard of ghee before doing a Whole30, but now I use it in many of my recipes. Originally from India, ghee is clarified butter whose milk solids have been strained out, which is why it's allowed on Whole30 and is a great dairy-free butter substitute. I have found it at Walmart and most natural food stores, though I also share three easy and budget-friendly ways to make it yourself on page 266.
- **COCONUT AMINOS:** Made from fermented coconut sap, this savory, salty seasoning sauce is a common swap for soy sauce and is allowed on Whole30. And no, it doesn't taste like coconut.
- **SALT:** All the recipes in this cookbook use basic iodized salt, or table salt, unless otherwise indicated. Adjust to taste if you are using a different salt.
- **OIL:** I often indicate, especially for my dressings, using an "extra-light-tasting" olive oil. Olive oil is excellent in dressings, and the extra-light taste helps keep the sauce more neutrally flavored so your mayo doesn't taste like olives.
- **VANILLA EXTRACT:** Pure vanilla extract is always ideal because it has fewer ingredients and better flavor. But as of this writing, that costs twenty dollars a bottle and is not affordable for us. Imitation vanilla extract will be slightly less flavorful but still works if that's what is accessible to you.
- **COCONUT WRAPS:** We don't use these often, but this is a Paleo tortilla-like option we use to make my Easy Egg Rolls (page 113) or sandwich wraps. These are made of coconut meat, water, and oil; are low-carb; and are

shelf stable for about a year. We find them at our local natural food store or on Amazon.

- **RAISINS:** For all recipes in this book that call for raisins, no-sugar-added dark raisins are preferred.

Kitchen Tools

You already know I live on a budget, so I can't afford to buy every kitchen tool out there. Here are some of my favorites that have been worth the cost for me. *None of these are required to be successful with this book or in the kitchen in general.*

- **HIGH-SPEED BLENDER:** I used a twenty-dollar blender for most of my adult life. But I got frustrated that my homemade hummus or pudding would still be a bit chunky. It was eventually worth it to me to get a Vitamix during a Black Friday sale, and I haven't looked back. It's a good investment for how fast and powerful it is and the incredible smooth results it provides. This investment will make an unbelievable difference in the creaminess of your puddings, soups, ice creams, and sauces; and it makes hidden veggies all the less noticeable!
- **AIR FRYER:** I adore my air fryer, and I'm kind of known for it. On my blog, *Whole Food for 7*, I go on and on about which ones I've had and why I love them. Why? Because an air fryer is *king* for crispy results. It's also a game-changer for leftovers because it can crisp day-old veggies and dishes without drying them out. Many of my recipes have an air fryer option, but they can also be made in the oven or on the stovetop.
- **SHARP KNIFE:** I don't know a ton about knives, and I don't have a lot of them. But after years of using a cheap set that we bought in college, I finally got a fifty-dollar knife and, wow, does it make a difference in speed and ease of prep! I have two chef's knives that I use and sharpen regularly, and that's made meal prepping so much faster.
- **FOOD PROCESSOR:** These make chopping a breeze, and they are great for blending, too.
- **IMMERSION BLENDER:** This handheld blender costs fifteen to twenty dollars and makes pureeing a snap, especially homemade mayo! There are ways to make mayo with a standing mixer or blender, but they can be tricky. This is a small investment that can help you save money in the long term as you make more homemade sauces and have more consistent and successful results.

- **MANDOLINE SLICER:** This is a helpful tool to slice fruits and veggies in thin, even slices. Ranging in price from ten to forty dollars, mandolines are great for making homemade Baked Apple Chips (page 184) or Plantain Chips (page 164) or thin slices of potato for my Whole30 Lasagna (page 122).
- **ICE CREAM MAKER:** OK, this is definitely not a must-have item, but, oh, do we love ours! It has been a gadget that I use way more than I expected and get asked about constantly. I have a Cuisinart model that is super easy to use and makes the creamiest homemade Paleo ice cream.

Easy Ways to Start the Day

1 CHAPTER

Hash Brown or Cauliflower Waffles

WHOLE 30   	SERVES:	PREP TIME:	COOK TIME:
	4	5 minutes	20 minutes

▾ **Note: Don't have a waffle iron? These can also be made into fritters. Combine the ingredients as directed below. In a medium saucepan, heat ¼ inch coconut or avocado oil over medium-high heat. Once oil is hot, scoop ¼ cup of mixture per fritter into pan. Flatten each fritter as it cooks in the pan so they crisp nicely and cook through. Cook until golden brown, or 3 to 4 minutes, then flip and cook 3 to 4 minutes more.**

This savory twist on a waffle is easy and fast. These are a great simple go-to for a busy morning or breakfast for dinner, and I love that I can sneak in some frozen veggies. I prefer to make these for my family with half store-bought hash browns and half cauliflower in the batter because my boys don't notice the cauliflower that way. If it's just going to be me and my hubby enjoying them, we love these with just cauliflower (no hash browns) for a delicious, nutrient-dense way to start the day.

3 cups store-bought frozen shredded hash browns or frozen riced cauliflower (or a mixture of both)
3 large eggs
¼ cup extra-virgin olive oil
¼ cup tapioca or arrowroot flour
1 teaspoon garlic salt
½ teaspoon onion powder
Optional: Salsa, dairy-free sour cream, bacon, green onion, ketchup, or sauce of choice, for topping

1 Preheat a nonstick waffle iron.

2 In a medium bowl, combine the hash browns, cauliflower, or a mixture of both. Add the eggs, oil, flour, garlic salt, and onion powder. Stir until the mixture is well combined.

3 Fill the preheated waffle iron with the batter; the exact amount will vary based on the size of your waffle iron. Keep in mind that this batter doesn't rise or spread as much as regular waffle

recipe continues

Leftover waffles can be frozen in a single layer then stored in a sealed container in the freezer for up to 3 months. Reheat the frozen waffles in a waffle iron, microwave, oven, or air fryer.

batter does, so you will probably need more batter than normal. In my 7-inch Belgian waffle iron, I use 1½ packed cups. If your batter is cauliflower only, really pack the cups so your waffles hold together. If your waffles are sticking, spray your waffle iron with cooking spray before making the next batch.

4 Close the waffle iron and cook until the waffle is crispy or your waffle maker indicates they are done. Timing will vary by iron.

5 Top with salsa, dairy-free sour cream, ketchup, or your sauce of choice and enjoy hot.

Loaded Breakfast Potatoes

WHOLE 30   

SERVES:	PREP TIME:	COOK TIME:
6	15 minutes	40 minutes

Time-Saving Tip: When I'm pressed for time, I swap the fresh potatoes, peppers, and onions for 2½ pounds of frozen potatoes O'Brien (small, cubed potatoes with peppers and onions already in the mix). Combine all the ingredients in one large saucepan over medium-high heat and cook until crispy. So easy!

This hearty breakfast keeps my boys full and well fueled for the whole morning. It goes so quickly in our house, we have to portion it so everyone gets some! For extra protein, you can add some scrambled eggs to the pan after the potatoes are crispy, cooking until set. Or you can serve the potatoes topped with cooked eggs to stretch the servings. This recipe is very flexible, and you can vary the breakfast meat used based on your family's preferences and what you have on hand.

½ pound ham, chopped into small ½-inch pieces
½ pound bacon, chopped into small ½-inch pieces
2 pounds Yukon gold potatoes, diced into ½-inch pieces
2 tablespoons coconut oil, melted, or other high-heat cooking oil
2 teaspoons garlic salt
2 cups finely chopped fresh or thawed frozen peppers and onions (I like using a food processor for this.)
Optional: Salsa or ketchup, for serving

1 In a large saucepan over medium heat, cook the ham and bacon until crispy, 17 to 18 minutes.

2 While the meat is cooking, place the potatoes in a 2- or 3-quart glass dish and add ¼ cup water. Cover with microwave-safe plastic wrap and steam in the microwave for 6 minutes, until the potatoes are tender and easily pierced with a fork or knife. (Or use your preferred steaming method.) Drain the water and pat the potatoes dry. Set aside.

recipe continues

Loaded Breakfast Potatoes,
continued

Freeze in a sealed container for up to 3 months.

3 When meat is browned, transfer it to a bowl. In the saucepan, place the oil and increase the heat to medium-high. Add the chopped potatoes in a single layer and sprinkle with the garlic salt. Let the mixture cook for 10 minutes without stirring, allowing the potatoes to get crispy. Flip the mixture, top with the peppers and onions, and cook for another 10 minutes, until the veggies are tender and the potatoes are crispy.

4 Add the ham and bacon to the pan and serve hot. My boys enjoy it served with salsa or ketchup.

Vanilla Granola

SERVES:	PREP TIME:	COOK TIME:
8*	5 minutes	1 hour

*MAKES: 8 cups

Note: For the chopped nuts, I like to use up whatever I have in my pantry, which is usually almonds, walnuts, cashews, or even coconut flakes. And while this is the basic formula, you can play around with variations such as adding dried cranberries or raisins, cocoa nibs, or chocolate chips. Just keep in mind that the total measurement of mix-ins plus the oats and/or nuts needs to be 5 cups. So if you want to add ½ cup raisins, the oats and/or nuts should measure 4½ cups. You can add a tablespoon of cinnamon or pumpkin pie spice to vary the flavor as well.

My boys used to live on cold cereal and milk. They ate it at least twice a day, going through a gallon of milk a day. When we switched to a gluten-free/dairy-free life, that was one of the things they really missed—and I missed how easy it was. There are quite a few gluten-free granolas available in stores now, which is fantastic. But many of them are either pricey or they have a long list of ingredients with lots of added sugar.

This granola recipe is flexible and so delicious. You can easily adapt it based on your dietary needs or preferences. Use oats for a nut-free version or just nuts for a Paleo version. I use my food processor to chop the nuts so that they're even and small, about the size of an oatmeal flake. My boys love this with the coconut sugar, but you can leave it out if you prefer a less sweet option.

2½ cups old-fashioned oats
2½ cups finely chopped nuts (see Note)
¼ cup coconut sugar or maple sugar
¼ teaspoon salt (skip if you are using salted nuts)
⅓ cup honey
⅓ cup extra-light-tasting olive oil or coconut oil, melted
1 tablespoon vanilla extract

1 Preheat the oven to 250°F. Line a baking sheet with parchment paper and set aside.

2 In a large bowl, combine the oats and/or nuts, sugar, and salt. Drizzle with the honey, oil, and vanilla and stir well until thoroughly combined.

recipe continues

Vanilla Granola,
continued

3 Spread mixture over the prepared baking sheet. Place another piece of parchment paper on top of the mixture and press it down firmly all over. This helps the mixture stick together, resulting in those nice, big chunks of granola. Discard the top piece of parchment.

4 Bake for 1 hour, or until the granola is light brown. Let the granola cool in the pan, then break it apart into chunks. Store the granola in an airtight container at room temperature for up to 3 weeks.

You can also freeze it for up to 3 months in a sealed container or reusable zip-top bag.

Just-Add-Water Paleo Pancake Mix

SERVES:	PREP TIME:	COOK TIME:
6*	10 minutes	15 minutes

*MAKES: 2 cups of mix (1 cup of mix yields 6 [4-inch] pancakes)

Note: You can leave out the coconut milk powder in the mix and just add ½ cup dairy-free milk to 1 cup of the batter instead. For a nut-free option, use 1 cup cassava flour in place of the tapioca, almond, and coconut flours. Mix 1 cup cassava mix with 6 tablespoons water.

Just-add-water pancake mixes are an easy breakfast solution I missed when we went gluten- and dairy-free. Not only does this recipe bring back that simple option, but it is also less expensive than the store-bought Paleo mixes. These pancakes are quick to make on a busy morning and straightforward enough for my boys to prepare themselves. I usually make a triple batch of mix and keep it in our pantry, and we love taking some when we travel or go camping. This is a versatile base you can use with a variety of pancake flavors and toppings. Want added nutrients and satiety? Add 2 tablespoons of collagen powder to the mix! I get the coconut milk powder from Amazon.

½ cup tapioca flour (see Note)
1 cup almond flour (see Note)
¼ cup coconut flour (see Note)
1 tablespoon baking powder
½ teaspoon salt
¼ cup coconut sugar
½ cup coconut milk powder (see Note)

1 In a medium bowl, combine the flours, baking powder, salt, sugar, and milk powder. Stir to combine. At this point, you can store the mix at room temperature in a sealed zip-top bag or container for up to 6 months.

2 To make a batch of pancakes, heat a large skillet over medium heat and spray lightly with cooking spray. Combine 1 cup of the mix with 6 tablespoons water and immediately pour 2 tablespoons batter per pancake into the pan. The coconut flour

recipe continues

will thicken once the water is added, and you will get the fluffiest pancakes if this thickening happens on the pan instead of in the bowl.

3 Flip the pancakes when the edges look set. Keep in mind that pancake thickness is all about the consistency of the batter. Pancakes too thick? Add 1 to 2 tablespoons water to the batter. Pancakes too thin? Add 1 to 2 tablespoons more pancake mix.

To freeze, lay the pancakes in a single layer and freeze. Store in a sealed zip-top bag or container for up to 6 months.

Build-Your-Own Tater Tot Egg Bites

WHOLE 30  	SERVES: 12*	PREP TIME: 15 minutes	COOK TIME: 30 minutes

*MAKES: 12 bites

Whole30 Option: If you are on a Whole30, no commercially prepared tater tots are allowed. Use equal amounts of compatible frozen shredded hash browns instead. Toss hash browns with ¼ cup olive or avocado oil before scooping ¼ cup hash browns into the prepared muffin cups. Press down and prepare the rest as explained above.

Egg bakes or frittatas are such an easy way to feed a crowd, but my boys were never into them. I finally convinced them to embrace these baked egg bites by using tater tots as the crust and letting them personalize it with their favorite fillings. Getting your kids involved in making the food can make them more willing to try it!

10-ounce bag frozen tater tots
8 large eggs, beaten
¼ cup dairy-free milk of choice
1 teaspoon salt
½ teaspoon ground black pepper
½ to 1 cup each fillings of choice: cooked bacon or sausage, chopped veggies, or dairy-free cheese
Optional: Salsa, ketchup, or hot sauce, for serving

1 Preheat the oven to 425°F. Spray a muffin tin pan with cooking spray.

2 Arrange 3 tater tots in the bottom of each muffin cup and bake for 10 minutes, until the tots are golden brown.

3 While the crust is baking, in a medium bowl, combine the eggs, milk, salt, and pepper. Set out all the filling options on the counter if the kids are building their own.

4 When the tater tots have finished baking, remove the pan from the oven, leaving the oven on. Use the bottom of a glass or the back of a spoon to flatten the tots into a crust. Top each crust with up to ¼ cup of toppings, followed by about 3 tablespoons scrambled eggs, or enough batter to just cover the toppings.

Freeze cooled egg bites in a sealed container for up to 3 months.

I find it easiest to do this with a liquid measuring cup that has a pour spout. Do not fill the muffin cups more than three-quarters full with egg or it will overflow as it cooks.

5 Bake for 25 to 30 minutes, until the eggs have set. Enjoy topped with salsa, ketchup, or hot sauce, if desired.

Breakfast Tacos or Burritos

WHOLE 30   	SERVES: 6	PREP TIME: 45 minutes*	COOK TIME: 50 minutes**

*PREP TIME: 25 minutes plus 20 minutes to prep tortillas
**COOK TIME: 30 minutes plus 20 minutes to cook tortillas

This hearty breakfast is a fantastic way to fill you up, and it happens to be my youngest son's favorite food of all time. After eating these for the first time, one of my boys said, "Wow, I am actually FULL!" These are delicious with my Cassava Flour Tortillas and also work great on a Whole30 as a breakfast taco with lettuce cups or as a breakfast burrito bowl with my Cilantro Lime Ranch (page 252) on top. If you can't eat eggs, these are delicious without them. In fact, a few of my boys prefer them that way. I love how customizable these are! If you can, I recommend making the tortillas the night before to make this a faster breakfast option.

Note: If modifying for Whole30, I highly recommend drizzling your lettuce cups or burrito bowls with my Cilantro Lime Ranch (page 252).

12 pieces bacon
2 tablespoons coconut or avocado oil
1 pound Yukon gold potatoes, diced
1 pound ground meat of choice
1 batch Taco Seasoning Mix (page 255)
1 batch burrito-sized Cassava Flour Tortillas (page 244), or store-bought GF tortillas, or lettuce leaves if preferred or modifying for a Whole30
10 large eggs, beaten (optional)
1 cup salsa
Optional: 1 cup dairy-free cheese, for serving

1 Line a baking sheet with parchment paper and lay the bacon on the pan. Place the bacon in a *cold* oven and set the temperature to 450°F. (This prevents the bacon from curling.) Bake for 20 minutes.

2 While the bacon cooks, in a medium saucepan over medium heat, melt the oil. Add the potatoes and cook until crispy, about 20 minutes. (The crispy potatoes are the best part!)

3 In another medium saucepan over medium heat, combine the ground meat and taco seasoning. Cook the meat until it is no longer pink inside, using a spoon to break it up as it cooks, about 10 minutes. Transfer the meat to a bowl and set aside.

4 If you haven't made the tortillas yet, make them now.

5 To minimize dishes, spray the saucepan you used for the meat with cooking spray. Over medium heat, cook the eggs until set, stirring occasionally, about 10 minutes.

To freeze, individually wrap each finished burrito in foil and then freeze in a sealed container for up to 3 months.

6 Set out all the ingredients (seasoned meat, potatoes, bacon, salsa, and cheese) and let everyone build their own burritos. If using cheese, I recommend you place it on the bottom, but there's no right way to layer these. To wrap the burritos, fold up the bottom and top edges and then tuck in one side around the filling before rolling tight.

Optional: Heat a skillet over medium heat and place the wrapped burritos seam-side down to cook for 3 to 4 minutes, until crisp. Repeat on the other side to melt the cheese (if using).

Crispy Paleo Waffles

SERVES:	PREP TIME:	COOK TIME:
6	15 minutes	15 minutes

▾ **Note: Can't do coconut or nuts? Use oat milk and maple sugar. Can't find cassava flour? You can also use 1 cup almond flour + 1 cup tapioca flour + ½ cup coconut flour. This is a great low-carb option, too. Also feel free to add ingredients like blueberries or dairy-free chocolate chips to the batter. I've included my favorite double-chocolate variation below.**

Growing up, my dad made these when I was a child. Homemade waffles and strawberries were on the menu for every holiday and birthday, so I knew that I had to create a gluten- and dairy-free version. We make these weekly, and my kids look forward to them every Monday. There are two flour options for these depending on what you have available and what works best for your dietary needs. Also, I challenge you to think outside the waffle—these make a fantastic affordable substitute for gluten-free bread! We use them like buns for sloppy joes, egg salad sandwiches, or breakfast sandwiches.

2 large eggs, carefully separated into whites and yolks
1½ cups almond milk or other dairy-free milk
2 cups cassava flour, plus more if needed (see Note)
½ cup extra-light-tasting olive oil
1 tablespoon baking powder
1 tablespoon coconut sugar, or other granulated sweetener such as monk fruit sugar (see Note)
1 teaspoon salt
Optional: pure maple syrup, ghee, nuts, berries, Whipped Coconut Cream (page 288), nut butter or Chocolate Nut Butter (page 262), for serving

1 Preheat a waffle iron.

2 In a medium bowl using a handheld mixer or in a standing mixer, beat the egg whites until stiff peaks form, 2 to 3 minutes. You might feel this step is too "fussy" and be tempted to skip it. Don't! It gives the waffles their great texture.

recipe continues

Crispy Paleo Waffles,
continued

3 In a large bowl, combine the egg yolks, almond milk, cassava flour, oil, baking powder, coconut sugar, and salt and stir until the mixture is smooth. The batter should have the consistency of cake batter. If it is too drippy/runny or not holding together as it cooks, add a little more flour, 1 or 2 tablespoons at a time. If the batter is too thick—more like a brownie batter—and the waffles are too dense, stir in more milk 1 tablespoon at a time. These should be light and crispy!

4 Gently fold in the egg whites. The batter will be on the lumpy side, but don't be tempted to overmix.

5 Cook the batter in your waffle iron per the manufacturer's instructions. The number of waffles you make will depend on the size of your iron. My 7-inch-diameter Belgian waffle pan makes 5 waffles. Due to the higher oil content in this recipe, I find that I don't need cooking spray. But if your waffles stick to your iron, spray your iron with cooking spray between batches.

6 Enjoy your waffles topped with maple syrup, ghee, nuts, berries, coconut whip cream, or nut butter.

To freeze, lay the waffles in a single layer on a cooling rack and freeze. Once frozen, store together in a sealed container for up to 3 months. Toast or microwave straight from the freezer to reheat. Great for fast breakfasts or after-school snack!

Double-Chocolate Waffle

Add 1 tablespoon vanilla to the batter, increase the coconut sugar to 3 tablespoons, and swap out ⅓ cup of the flour with cocoa powder (so 1⅔ cups cassava flour + ⅓ cup cocoa). Add ⅓ cup dairy-free chocolate chips to make them "double" chocolate, if desired. We prefer the Enjoy Life mini chips.

Breakfast Salad

WHOLE 30   

SERVES:	PREP TIME:	COOK TIME:
4	5 minutes	25 minutes

▾ **Note: The homemade chicken apple sausage is also great on its own; just shape it into small round patties and cook in a saucepan as otherwise directed below. I use my mini food processor to chop the apple, skin on, into small pieces. You can also use a store-bought chicken apple sausage, chopped and browned, for a faster option.**

At my first Whole30 Coaches Summit, the resort served a breakfast salad. It was something I had never thought of before! Whole30 encourages having a plate full of veggies at every meal, but veggies for breakfast takes a little outside-of-the-box thinking. This breakfast salad combines some breakfast favorites like hash browns and bacon with greens plus a sweet dressing to make a dish that my hubby and I will fight over. Feel free to put a cooked or scrambled egg on this!

FOR THE SAUSAGE:

1 pound ground chicken or turkey
⅔ cup finely chopped apple, variety of your choice
½ teaspoon dried sage
½ teaspoon dried thyme
½ teaspoon onion powder
½ teaspoon salt
½ teaspoon ground black pepper
1 tablespoon olive or avocado oil

FOR THE SALAD:

8 slices bacon
2 tablespoons olive or avocado oil
4 cups frozen hash browns
8 cups packed fresh baby arugula
2 medium fresh avocados, sliced
Creamy Apple Dressing (page 259)

1 **MAKE THE SAUSAGE:** In a medium bowl, combine the meat, apple, sage, thyme, onion powder, salt, and pepper. In a medium saucepan over medium heat, heat the oil then add the sausage mixture. Cook, stirring and mashing the mixture into small pieces with your spatula, until the meat is no longer pink inside, about 10 minutes. The apples might release water into the pan, so drain

recipe continues

any excess liquid, if needed, and then cook for 5 minutes more to brown. Set aside.

2 **MAKE THE SALAD:** To cook the bacon, line a baking sheet with parchment paper. If you have a cooling rack that fits inside your baking sheet, put that on top of the parchment. Lay out the bacon strips on the parchment or cooling rack. Put the tray into a *cold* oven and then turn on the oven to 425°F. Bake for 20 to 22 minutes, depending on desired crispness.

3 To cook the hash browns on the stove, in a medium saucepan, heat the oil over medium heat. Once hot, add the hash browns, flattening them into an even layer. Cook for 10 minutes, flip, and cook for 10 minutes more, until crispy and golden.

To cook the hash browns in an air fryer, toss the hash browns with the oil and spread them in the air fryer basket. Air fry at 400°F for 18 to 20 minutes, stirring halfway through.

4 Assemble the salads by dividing the arugula among four bowls. Top each evenly with the hash browns, sausage, bacon, and avocado. If eating the salads immediately, drizzle each with ¼ cup of the dressing. Otherwise, you can store the assembled salads in sealed containers in the fridge for a few days, waiting to cut the avocado and to toss them with the dressing until you're ready to eat.

Pink Starburst Smoothie

SERVES:	PREP TIME:	COOK TIME:
2 to 3	10 minutes	0 minutes

Note: If you find yourself with any leftover smoothie, you can freeze it in an ice cube tray and add the cubes to your next smoothie! If collagen powder isn't accessible, leave it out and serve with a protein side like my Homemade Breakfast Sausage (page 57) instead. You can substitute an equal amount of another dairy-free milk for the coconut milk as needed.

Smoothies are a classic solution for breakfast or a snack in a snap. The challenge is that they are often heavy on the fruit and light on any nutritional staying power. My boys were always hungry one to two hours after having traditional smoothies for breakfast. Over the years, I've discovered three secret weapons to use in our smoothies that I want to share through this recipe: (1) adding frozen cauliflower rice for thickness and a shockingly undetectable veggie (promise!), (2) adding protein through collagen powder, and (3) introducing healthy fats with coconut milk, which also makes these extra creamy!

2 cups frozen riced cauliflower
1 cup frozen raspberries
1 cup frozen strawberries
1 cup unsweetened apple juice
½ cup full-fat coconut milk
2 scoops collagen powder (see Note)
¼ cup honey
¼ cup lemon juice
1 tablespoon vanilla extract

In a blender, combine all the ingredients and blend until very smooth, 3 to 4 minutes. Enjoy immediately.

Homemade Breakfast Sausage

WHOLE 30

SERVES:	PREP TIME:	COOK TIME:
4	5 minutes	10 minutes

Whole30-compatible sausage can be hard to find and is sometimes pricey. But you can easily and affordably make your own with this sausage seasoning. It works well with any ground meat of your choice. My boys love it with pork, and my hubby loves it with ground chicken. These patties freeze well and are an awesome make-ahead staple to have on hand for a fast breakfast protein. I find these easiest to make on the stove, but you can also make them in the oven or air fryer.

1 pound ground meat of choice
1 teaspoon dried sage
½ teaspoon salt
½ teaspoon ground black pepper
¼ teaspoon garlic powder
¼ teaspoon onion powder
¼ teaspoon paprika
Pinch of ground nutmeg (optional)
1 tablespoon olive or avocado oil, if using a leaner meat like turkey or chicken

1 If baking the sausage, preheat the oven to 400°F. Line a baking sheet with parchment paper and set aside.

2 In a medium bowl, combine the meat with the sage, salt, pepper, garlic powder, onion powder, paprika, and nutmeg (if using). I find it easiest to do this with my hands, but you can also use a spatula.

3 With greased hands, shape the mixture into 1½-tablespoon patties.

recipe continues

4 If baking, arrange the patties in a single layer on the prepared baking sheet. Bake for 5 minutes, flip the patties, then broil on high for 4 to 5 minutes, until the patties are browned.

5 If making the patties on the stove, heat a large saucepan or skillet over medium heat. Pour in the oil (if using). Once the oil is hot, cook as many patties as will fit in the pan without crowding for 3 to 4 minutes on each side, until browned on the outside and no longer pink on the inside. Repeat with remaining patties.

Lay the patties in a single layer. You may need to do this in batches. Air fry at 350°F for 6 minutes. Increase the heat to 400°F and cook for 2 minutes more to brown the patties.

Freeze in a single layer on a cooling rack or baking pan lined with parchment. Once frozen, store together in a sealed container for up to 3 months.

Breakfast Bowl

WHOLE 30  	SERVES: 4	PREP TIME: 20 minutes	COOK TIME: 22 to 35 minutes*

*COOK TIME: 22 to 35 minutes, depending on cooking method

This veggie-packed breakfast bowl starts your day off with lots of nutrition and flavor. It's another delicious way to get those veggies in your morning meal. My husband said he would be OK if I made this every day of his Whole30. I steam the veggies first to shorten the roasting time, which is a great option when time is tight.

1 pound sweet potatoes (about 1 large potato), cut into small ½-inch cubes
1 pound fresh Brussels sprouts, halved or quartered if large
¼ cup extra-virgin olive or avocado oil
8 slices bacon
Cooking oil spray
10 large eggs
¼ cup almond milk or other dairy-free milk
½ teaspoon salt
½ teaspoon ground black pepper
2 large fresh avocados, sliced
Everything bagel seasoning (optional)

1 Preheat the oven to 425°F.

2 Steam the cut sweet potatoes and Brussels sprouts. I do this by adding the veggies and ¼ cup water to a steamable reusable bag like a Stasher bag, or to a large glass dish covered with microwavable saran wrap and microwaving for 5 minutes, or until tender.

3 In a large bowl, toss the steamed veggies with the oil and arrange them on a baking sheet. Roast for 30 minutes, until golden brown and crispy. Keep an eye on the vegetables as they

recipe continues

Breakfast Bowl,
continued

Air fry the veggies at 400°F for 17 to 18 minutes.

Freeze the roasted potatoes, Brussels sprouts, and bacon in a sealed container for up to 3 months. I don't recommend the texture of cooked scrambled eggs that have been frozen. Rather, quickly make those the morning of and then top with fresh avocado.

cook; the Brussels sprouts sometimes finish before the sweet potatoes.

4 In a skillet over medium heat, cook the bacon in batches, if necessary, while the veggies are roasting or air frying.

5 Spray a medium saucepan with cooking spray. In a medium bowl, whisk together the eggs, milk, salt, and pepper. In the prepared saucepan over medium heat, cook the egg mixture, stirring, until the eggs are set, 8 to 10 minutes.

6 Build your bowl by combining one-quarter of the roasted veggies and eggs, topped with 2 pieces of bacon, half an avocado, and sprinkle with everything bagel seasoning (optional).

Breakfast Taquitos

		SERVES: 6	PREP TIME: 20 minutes	COOK TIME: 20 minutes

Note: To make this recipe corn-free, you can use my Cassava Flour Tortillas (page 244), making them 6 inches wide and as thin as possible. Aim to slightly undercook them so they remain soft and pliable. You'll only need to cook the cassava flour tortilla taquitos in the oven for 15 minutes and in the air fryer for 10. Otherwise, they get too crunchy.

Taquito is Spanish for "small taco," and they are a Mexican food traditionally consisting of a small rolled-up tortilla with beef, cheese, or chicken filling and then fried. These are a fun, crispy, handheld breakfast option that is excellent as a make-ahead. They can be made in the air fryer or the oven, and you can vary the ingredients as desired. The taquitos are a real hit in my family. My oldest, who doesn't like eggs, enjoyed these, and they have become one of my youngest's all-time favorite breakfasts. I love to make a big batch on Sunday while I am cooking dinner, and my kids can reheat and eat them all week long.

½ pound chorizo or ½ pound ground meat of choice seasoned with 1 tablespoon Taco Seasoning Mix (page 255)
8 large eggs
¼ cup dairy-free milk of choice
1 teaspoon salt, plus more to taste
½ teaspoon ground black pepper
18 (5-inch) corn tortillas
1 cup dairy-free cheddar or pepper Jack cheese
Cooking oil spray
Optional: salsa

1 If making these in the oven, preheat the oven to 400°F and line a baking pan with parchment paper.

2 In a large saucepan over medium heat, cook the chorizo until it's no longer pink, about 10 minutes.

3 As the meat cooks, whisk together the eggs, milk, salt, and pepper. Once the meat is cooked, add the egg mixture to the meat and scramble until set, about 10 minutes.

recipe continues

4 Wrap the tortillas completely in damp paper towels and microwave until soft, about 1½ minutes. This will make them pliable so they won't break when wrapping the taquitos. Lay a large piece of parchment paper on the counter for easy cleanup as you get ready to assemble the taquitos.

5 **ASSEMBLE THE TAQUITOS:** Lay a warm tortilla on the parchment. Sprinkle it down the middle with 1 tablespoon of the cheese. Top with about 3 tablespoons of the meat and egg mixture. Take one edge of the tortilla parallel to the meat mixture and tuck it over and then just under the mixture tightly. Then continue rolling up the tortilla as tightly as you can. Place the taquito seam-side down. Repeat with all of the tortillas and meat mixture.

6 Spray the taquitos generously with cooking oil spray and sprinkle them lightly with salt, if desired. Bake for 20 minutes, until crispy. Serve with salsa, if desired.

Arrange the taquitos in a single layer in an air fryer basket. You will probably need to do this in batches. Spray the taquitos generously with cooking oil spray and sprinkle them lightly with salt, if desired. Air fry for 10 minutes at 375°F, until crispy.

Freeze in a sealed container for up to 3 months.

Breakfast Oat Cups

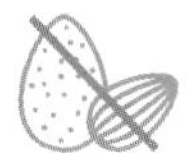

SERVES:	PREP TIME:	COOK TIME:
12*	15 minutes	15 minutes

*MAKES: 12 oat cups

▾ **Note: I recommend using steam-in-a-bag frozen cauliflower for this, though you could also use leftover cooked riced cauliflower. If you go the microwave route, make sure to cool the cauliflower before adding it to the batter, or it will melt the chocolate chips. If collagen powder isn't accessible, don't worry. These still work without that protein boost. To make the oat cups nut-free, use sun butter and ½ cup cassava flour instead of the almond and tapioca flours.**

I worked hard to make sure this recipe was not just tasty but also packed with good nutrition so my kids start the day on the right foot. Similar to muffins but a little denser, they mimic a brand of store-bought gluten-free oat cups my kids love. These freeze well for an awesome grab-and-go option. And, no, my boys have no idea there is cauliflower in them. You can use either quick or old-fashioned oats in these. With veggies, protein, and healthy fats, these are a satiating, delicious beginning to the day!

Nonstick cooking oil spray
1 cup steamed riced cauliflower, cooled (see note)
¼ cup nut or seed butter (see Note)
¼ cup honey
2 tablespoons extra-light-tasting olive oil or melted coconut oil
1 teaspoon vanilla extract
2 large eggs
1 cup uncooked oats
¾ cup almond flour (see Note)
¼ cup tapioca flour
2 tablespoons unflavored protein or collagen powder
1 teaspoon baking powder
½ teaspoon salt
¼ cup dairy-free mini chocolate chips

1. Preheat the oven to 350°F. Spray a muffin tin with nonstick cooking oil spray and set aside.

2. In a food processor or blender, combine the cauliflower, nut butter, honey, oil, vanilla, and eggs and blend until well mixed.

3. Add the oats, flours, protein powder, baking powder, and salt and blend again until combined. Transfer the mixture to a large

recipe continues

bowl and gently fold in the chocolate chips. The batter will not be very thick.

Freeze the oat cups in a single layer until solid, then store in a sealed reusable zip-top bag or sealed container for up to 3 months.

4 Spoon about ¼ cup of batter into each cup of the prepared muffin pan. Bake for 20 to 23 minutes, until the tops of the oat cups spring back when gently pressed. Let the oat cups cool on a cooling rack or on the counter for 5 minutes before eating.

Home-Run Kid Favorites

2 CHAPTER

Our Favorite Chicken Strips

WHOLE 30   

SERVES:	PREP TIME:	COOK TIME:
4	45 minutes	10 to 20 minutes*

*COOK TIME: 10 to 20 minutes, depending on cooking method

Note: If you don't like pickles or can't find compatible ones, you can omit this ingredient; they will taste more like popcorn chicken. I don't like pickles, but I don't mind the subtle flavor here, and the juice makes the chicken so tender.

Can't do egg? You can use ¼ cup dairy-free milk instead. I find the thickness of canned coconut milk works best. Can't do nuts? You can substitute 2 tablespoons coconut flour instead of the almond flour, or you can omit the almond flour and use more tapioca or arrowroot flour. The breading won't turn out as thick, but it'll still be tasty.

Lastly, while these are technically Whole30-compatible, they could be too close to old habits, especially if KFC was your *thing* before Whole30. Please use some personal responsibility in deciding if these are right for your Whole30.

Our favorite fast-food chicken strips come from a famous chain that's known for only selling chicken. My boys were dying for me to re-create this at home, and now they love it even more than the restaurant's version! I love it more, too, since I can replace a long list of unhealthy additives and they freeze fantastically. This was also the first recipe my then-thirteen-year-old learned how to make himself. We prefer the juiciness of these cooked on the stove, but you can make them in the air fryer, too.

1 pound boneless, skinless chicken breasts, cut into strips or nuggets
½ cup pickle juice (see Note)
1 large egg (see Note)
⅓ cup almond flour (see Note)
¼ cup tapioca or arrowroot flour
1 teaspoon salt
¾ teaspoon paprika
½ teaspoon garlic powder
¼ teaspoon onion powder
¼ teaspoon ground black pepper
Coconut or avocado oil, for cooking
Optional: Whole30 Date Mustard Sauce (page 250), for serving

1. In a medium bowl, combine the chicken breasts and pickle juice. Cover and let the chicken marinate in the fridge for at least 30 minutes or overnight. The longer you let it marinate, the stronger the pickle flavor will be.

2. Drain and discard the pickle juice. (A strainer works well here.) Pat the chicken dry to help breading stick. Set the chicken aside.

3. In a small bowl, lightly whisk the egg. Pour the egg into the bowl with the chicken and stir until all of the pieces are coated.

recipe continues

Drain off any excess egg, again using a strainer. Shake the strainer a few times to encourage any extra egg to drain. Transfer the chicken to a medium bowl.

4 In a small bowl, stir together the almond flour, tapioca flour, salt, paprika, garlic powder, onion powder, and pepper. Sprinkle the breading mixture over the chicken and gently stir to make sure all of the chicken is coated.

5 In a medium saucepan over medium-high heat, pour in about ¼ inch of oil. Once hot, carefully place the chicken into the oil, taking care not to crowd the pan. You may need to do this in batches. Cook the chicken for 5 to 6 minutes per side, until crispy and golden brown. Repeat until all of the pieces are cooked through with no pink inside.

Cook the chicken at 350°F for 10 minutes, flipping halfway through.

These make great substitutes for frozen chicken nuggets. After the chicken is cooked, lay the pieces in a single layer on a cooling rack or pan lined with parchment to freeze. Once frozen, store in a sealed container for up to 3 months. You can reheat the nuggets in the microwave, in the oven at 400°F for 10 minutes, or in the air fryer at 350°F for 5 to 7 minutes. *Want them cooked fresh?* You can also freeze these raw just after you've breaded them, and then cook them on the stove or in the air fryer straight from the freezer with the above cooking instructions, adding a few minutes cooking time.

Make It a Meal

We love these paired with my Breaded Potato Wedges (page 227), Onion Rings (page 212) or Caulitots (page 219), Broccoli Salad (page 215), and my Whole30 Date Mustard Sauce (page 250).

Plantain Pizza Pockets

WHOLE 30   	SERVES: 6*	PREP TIME: 40 minutes	COOK TIME: 30 minutes

*MAKES: 6 pockets

Note: Success with this one-ingredient dough is all about the temperature. If the dough gets too hot, it will break apart. If it gets too cold, it will no longer be pliable. Use the fridge as directed to cool the dough for 10 minutes but not longer. Once you start working with the dough, do so from start to finish.

Make It a Meal

These pair great with my Caesar Salad (page 204, sans chicken) and Creamy Fruit Salad (page 234).

This recipe is an absolute win-win. My boys have been begging me to make a healthier pizza pocket for years, and they can't get enough of these. I'm thrilled to have found a "dough" solution that is only one ingredient! My love for tostones inspired me to try this plantain-based dough, and it does not disappoint, even with its simple, singular ingredient. Though it takes a little time to roll out the dough and form each pocket, it's so worth it, and we have these on repeat in our house.

The filling possibilities are endless! Ham and cheese, eggs and bacon, taco meat—get creative. Just make sure to use green plantains, not yellow, or the dough won't get crispy.

2 pounds green plantains
1 cup chopped pepperoni or other pizza toppings of choice
1 cup Pantry Marinara Sauce (page 268) or store-bought
¼ cup dairy-free mozzarella cheese (optional)
Tapioca or arrowroot flour, as needed
Extra-virgin olive oil, as needed

1 Fill a large pot with 3 inches of water. Bring it to a boil over high heat. While the water is coming to a boil, peel the plantains and cut into roughly 1-inch chunks. Green plantain peels can be a little tough to get off; I do so by trimming off the ends of the plantain and cutting the plantain in half. I score down the side of the peel to create a place to start lifting the peel away from the fruit with my thumb, then I continue to peel off the rest.

2 Place the peeled plantain chunks into the boiling water and boil for 10 minutes, until very tender. Strain the plantain and

recipe continues

Plantain Pizza Pockets,
continued

transfer the pieces to a food processor or blender. Blend until smooth, scraping down the sides of the blender or food processor bowl as needed. It should form a creamy, slightly sticky dough. Transfer the dough to the fridge to cool for 10 minutes.

3. Meanwhile, in a medium bowl, combine the pepperoni, marinara sauce, and cheese (if using). Set aside.

4. Preheat the oven to 425°F. Line a baking sheet with parchment paper and set aside.

5. Sprinkle the counter or a bread board with the flour. Flour your hands and roughly divide the dough into 6 balls. Coat each ball with flour on all sides and then roll them out into a circle about ¼ inch thick. If the dough starts breaking apart and becomes hard to handle, let it cool in the fridge for 5 minutes more.

6. On one-half of a dough circle, scoop ¼ cup of sauce and topping mixture, leaving a ¼-inch border around the edge to create the seal. Fold the empty side of the dough over the top of the topping mixture. Seal the pocket by crimping the dough with your fingers. Place the pizza pocket on the prepared baking sheet. Repeat with the remaining dough and sauce. Brush the tops of the pockets generously with olive oil to coat.

7. Bake for 30 minutes, until the pockets are crispy and golden on the outside. Serve immediately.

Cook at 350°F in a single layer for 15 minutes, or until golden.

Freeze the pockets in a single layer on a tray or baking sheet. Store in a sealed container for up to 3 months.

Tostones Nachos

WHOLE 30  	SERVES: 6	PREP TIME: 20 minutes	COOK TIME: 30 minutes*

*COOK TIME: 15 minutes to assemble Nachos, 10 minutes for the Easy Whole30 Guacamole, 5 minutes for the Easy Whole30 Blender Salsa

My best friend and I have thirteen children between us (!). Recently, we went on a kid-free beach vacation to Santa Cruz complete with sunshine, bike rides, and amazing food. One of my favorite meals was an incredible plate of loaded nachos from a restaurant right on the beach. It was dream-worthy food, and I was thrilled to re-create it at home with this recipe. This is a great family dish because we set out the ingredients buffet-style and let the kids choose what they want. They pair well with sides of my Cilantro Lime Rice or Caulirice (page 133) and Cilantro Salsa Slaw (page 243).

2 tablespoons olive or avocado oil, if using chicken breasts
1 pound ground meat of choice or boneless, skinless chicken breasts, cut into 1-inch pieces
1 batch Taco Seasoning Mix (page 255)
1 batch Tostones (page 224) or store-bought tostones or chips (not Whole30)
1 batch Easy Whole30 Guacamole (recipe follows), or store-bought
1 batch Easy Whole30 Blender Salsa (recipe follows), or store-bought
1 batch Nacho Cheese Sauce (page 257)
Optional: Chopped fresh cilantro, diced jalapeños, drained and rinsed black beans,* corn*

1 In a large saucepan, heat the oil over medium heat if using chicken. Add the chicken or ground meat (no oil) and sprinkle with the taco seasoning. Cook for 10 minutes, until the meat is cooked through and no longer pink in the center.

(*not Whole30-compatible)

recipe continues

2 You can either build the nachos on a large platter and serve them family-style or let everyone build their own. If serving family-style, I start with the tostones on the bottom then layer with guac, meat, salsa, cheese sauce, cilantro, and jalapeños (if using).

Easy Whole30 Guacamole

In a medium bowl, mash and combine the flesh of 3 ripe avocados, ½ teaspoon garlic powder, ¼ teaspoon onion powder, ¼ teaspoon salt, and a pinch of ground cumin. Once mashed to your desired consistency, add 1 cup finely chopped fresh cilantro.

Easy Whole30 Blender Salsa

In a food processor or blender, pulse 1 white onion with 1 cup packed fresh cilantro for 1 minute to chop. Add 1 (15-ounce) can diced tomatoes, 1 (10-ounce) can diced tomatoes with green chiles, 1 teaspoon garlic powder, ¾ teaspoon salt, and a pinch of ground cumin. Pulse a few times until the mixture reaches your desired consistency.

Crispy Honey Garlic Chicken

WHOLE 30   

SERVES:	PREP TIME:	COOK TIME:
4	20 minutes	15 to 25 minutes*

*COOK TIME: 15 to 25 minutes, depending on cooking method

Note: For an egg-free dish, you can use ½ cup canned coconut milk instead of the eggs. For a Whole30 glaze, use 3 tablespoons Date Paste (page 269) and 2 tablespoons of water instead of the honey.

Make It a Meal

This is delicious with my Broccoli Salad (page 215) or Balsamic Brussels Sprouts (page 233), Roasted Potatoes (page 121), and Cloud Drop Biscuits (page 223, not Whole30)

This crispy glazed chicken has fast become a favorite in our home—the kind that my kids cheer for when they hear it's coming to the table. You don't need many ingredients for this, and most are pantry staples. We prefer the extra-crispy result from this cooked on the stove, but you can also make this in an air fryer or oven. Sweet and crispy with a touch of garlic, this chicken is a home run!

FOR THE CHICKEN:

- **1 pound boneless, skinless chicken breasts, fat trimmed**
- **½ cup tapioca or arrowroot flour**
- **1½ teaspoons paprika**
- **1 teaspoon garlic salt**
- **1 teaspoon ground black pepper**
- **2 large eggs (see Note)**
- **½ cup coconut oil or other high-heat oil**

FOR THE HONEY GARLIC GLAZE:

- **1 tablespoon extra-virgin olive oil**
- **1 tablespoon minced fresh garlic**
- **2 tablespoons coconut aminos**
- **¼ cup plus 2 tablespoons honey (see Note)**

1 **MAKE THE CHICKEN:** Cut trimmed chicken breasts in half lengthwise, creating long, thin chicken breast pieces. Set aside.

2 In a small bowl, combine the flour, paprika, garlic salt, and pepper. In a separate small bowl, beat the eggs. Pat dry the chicken with a paper towel to help the breading adhere. Have a lightly floured plate or piece of parchment paper handy.

recipe continues

Crispy Honey Garlic Chicken,
continued

3 Press both sides of each chicken piece into the flour mixture, shaking off any excess. Next, coat both sides with egg, allowing any excess to drain off. Press the chicken into the flour mixture once again. Transfer the breaded chicken to the prepared plate or parchment and continue with the remaining chicken.

Spray the air fryer basket with cooking spray. Place the breaded chicken in the air fryer. Spray the chicken with cooking oil and then cook for 13 to 15 minutes at 350°F, flipping once halfway through.

4 In a medium skillet over medium heat, melt the coconut oil. Cook the chicken for 6 minutes on each side, or until outside is crispy and chicken is no longer pink inside.

5 While chicken is cooking, make the glaze. In a small saucepan, heat the olive oil over medium heat. Once hot, add the garlic and cook for 3 minutes, until fragrant and light brown. Remove from heat. In a small bowl, combine the garlic with the coconut aminos and honey, stirring to combine.

6 After the chicken is done cooking, brush the pieces with the glaze. My boys love using the leftover glaze as a dipping sauce! For a thicker sauce, chill it in the fridge before serving.

Note: You can also make this recipe in the oven. Preheat the oven to 425°F. Place a baking sheet in the oven as it preheats—the hot pan will help the chicken get crispy underneath. When ready to cook, line the baking sheet with parchment paper. Spray the chicken generously with cooking oil and cook for 15 minutes. Flip and cook for 10 minutes more.

Lay the unglazed chicken in a single layer and freeze. Store in a sealed container up to 3 months. Store the cooked glaze in a zip-top bag or container with the chicken.

Stuffed Waffles

			SERVES: 6	PREP TIME: 15 minutes	COOK TIME: 10 to 20 minutes*

*Cook time: 10 to 20 minutes, depending on the size of your waffle iron

Pictured on page 84

Great Paleo sandwiches are hard to come by, so why not use my Paleo waffles as the "bread" and add all kinds of fillings? These stuffed waffles are so easy to make and a huge hit in my house. I love how versatile they are with so many filling options! They also freeze well and are a fantastic and fast dinner, snack option, or make-ahead breakfast. My boys also enjoy them cold in their lunch boxes. It might take a few attempts for you to learn how much batter to use without overfilling your waffle maker, but it's so worth it.

1 batch Crispy Paleo Waffles batter (page 49)

FOR PIZZA-STUFFED WAFFLES:

48 slices pepperoni
1½ cups store-bought marinara sauce
1½ cups dairy-free mozzarella cheese

FOR HAM-AND-CHEESE-STUFFED WAFFLES:

12 slices thin deli ham
1½ cups dairy-free cheddar cheese

FOR FIESTA CHICKEN-STUFFED WAFFLES:

3 cups shredded cooked chicken
1½ cups salsa
3 tablespoons Taco Seasoning Mix (page 255)
1½ cups dairy-free cheddar cheese

FOR SAUSAGE-AND-EGG-STUFFED WAFFLES:

1 pound sausage, removed from the casing and cooked into crumbles
5 large eggs, scrambled and cut into small pieces
1½ cups dairy-free cheddar cheese (optional)

1 Prepare the waffle batter per the instructions. Preheat your waffle iron.

2 In a hot waffle iron, use a spatula to spread a thin layer of the waffle batter. (Use only as much as you need to just cover the waffle iron, or you will have waffle batter spilling out the sides. For example, my mini single waffle iron usually uses ¼ cup batter. That means I spread no more than 2 tablespoons of batter on the bottom and top.)

3 Layer your fillings of choice over the batter. Here is how much each individual waffle will use, which I cook in my 4-inch waffle iron, though this will vary based on the size of your waffle iron:

PIZZA WAFFLES = 4 slices pepperoni + 1 tablespoon sauce + 1 tablespoon cheese

HAM-AND-CHEESE WAFFLES = 1 slice ham (folded or cut if needed) + 1 tablespoon cheese

FIESTA CHICKEN WAFFLES = 2 tablespoons shredded chicken + 1 tablespoon salsa + ½ teaspoon taco seasoning + 1 tablespoon cheese

SAUSAGE-AND EGG-WAFFLES = 1 heaping tablespoon sausage + 1 heaping tablespoon scrambled eggs + 1 tablespoon cheese (if using)

4 Spread another thin layer of waffle batter over the filling ingredients. Cook according to your waffle iron instructions. Enjoy hot or freeze in a single layer for later. If freezing, once frozen, store in a sealed container for up to 3 months.

Confetti Nuggets

WHOLE 30					SERVES:	PREP TIME:	COOK TIME:
					6*	10 minutes	20 minutes

*MAKES: 18 nuggets

Pictured on page 85

Make It a Meal

Pair these nuggets with my Carrot Fries (page 216) or Breaded Potato Wedges (page 227) and Creamy Fruit Salad (page 234).

I love that these simple nuggets have a hearty dose of veggies in them. With minimal ingredients and prep, these are an awesome, straightforward main dish. Even my picky eater reached for seconds and had leftovers the next day for lunch. I use frozen steam-in-a-bag veggies and then my food processor to chop them finely for a more subtle veggie presence. We prefer mixed veggies for this, like a stir-fry blend or broccoli Normandy.

1 pound ground chicken or turkey
1 cup steamed veggies, chopped into fine pieces
3 tablespoons tapioca, arrowroot, or potato flour
1 teaspoon garlic salt
1 teaspoon onion powder
1 teaspoon paprika
Optional: Whole30 Date Mustard Sauce (page 250), for serving

1. Preheat the oven to 400°F. Line a baking sheet with parchment paper.

2. In a medium bowl, mix together the meat, veggies, flour, garlic salt, onion powder, and paprika. I find this easiest to do with my hands. Once combined, shape about 1 tablespoon of the mixture into a ball and place it on the prepared baking sheet. Gently flatten the ball with your hand so it takes on more of a nugget shape. Repeat with the remaining mixture.

3. Bake for 10 minutes, flip, and then broil on high for another 7 to 8 minutes, until browned. We love these with my Whole30 Date Mustard Sauce.

After cooking the nuggets, freeze them in a single layer. Store in a sealed container or zip-top bag for up to 3 months.

Generously spray the air fryer basket with cooking oil. After shaping the nuggets, place them in a single layer in the basket. Cook at 350°F for 8 to 10 minutes, until browned.

Taco Chicken Strips

WHOLE 30					SERVES: 4	PREP TIME: 15 minutes	COOK TIME: 8 to 15 minutes

Note: For those with egg allergies, you can use ½ cup canned coconut milk instead of the eggs. To make these Whole30-compatible, be sure to use my Plantain Chips (page 164), as no store-bought chips are allowed on Whole30. Or you can modify by using 1 cup almond flour instead of the crushed plantain chips. To get the best crumb from your plantain chips, use a food processor or put the chips in a reusable zip-top bag and crush them with a kitchen mallet or other heavy object.

Make It a Meal

We love these paired with my Cilantro Lime Ranch (page 252) or Chipotle Mayo (page 253) as a dipping sauce, with my Cilantro Salsa Slaw (page 243) and Caulitots (page 219) on the side.

Two of our family's favorites unite in this delicious and fast entrée. We could eat Mexican food or chicken strips on the daily, so my family was thrilled to get both in these! You don't need a lot of ingredients for this to be a family hit, and the crushed plantain chip breading gives these an amazing texture.

1 pound boneless, skinless chicken breasts, trimmed of fat and cut into strips or nuggets
¼ cup tapioca or arrowroot flour
1 large egg (see Note)
2 tablespoons Taco Seasoning Mix (page 255)
2 cups Plantain Chips (page 164), crushed into fine crumbs (see Note)
Dipping sauce of choice, for serving (see Make It a Meal)

1. Preheat the oven to 350°F. Set a cooling rack on a baking sheet, spray the rack with cooking spray, and set aside. This is the best way to allow the chicken to cook most effectively on all sides. If you don't have a cooling rack, line a cookie sheet with parchment paper.

2. Set out three small bowls. In one, pour the flour. In the second, beat the egg. In the third, combine the taco seasoning and crushed plantain chips. Pat the chicken pieces dry using paper towels to help the breading adhere.

3. To bread the chicken pieces, coat both sides in the tapioca flour, shaking off any excess. Then lay the chicken in the egg, flip to coat both sides, and allow the excess to drip off. Finally, coat the chicken with the plantain-taco mixture, pressing the chicken

recipe continues

pieces firmly into the mixture. Lay the breaded chicken pieces on the prepared pan and repeat with the remaining chicken. Spray each breaded chicken piece with cooking spray.

Cook at 350°F for 8 to 9 minutes, shaking or flipping halfway through, until the chicken is no longer pink inside.

4 Cook for 12 to 15 minutes, flipping halfway through and spraying again with cooking spray, until the chicken is golden on the outside and cooked through with no pink inside. Cook time will depend on the size of your nuggets or strips.

Freeze in a single layer on a cooling rack or baking sheet lined with parchment. Once frozen, store in a sealed container for up to 3 months.

Orange Chicken

WHOLE 30

SERVES:	PREP TIME:	COOK TIME:
4	10 minutes	20 minutes

Make It a Meal

We enjoy this with broccoli or Crispy Freezer Veggies (page 247) and steamed cauliflower rice or white rice (not Whole30).

Orange chicken is a very Americanized version of the sweet and sour chicken dishes of China and a takeout favorite. Orange chicken is a variation of General Tso Chicken, a dish most commonly attributed to a Taiwanese chef in New York in the 1970s and was originally based on Hunanese cuisine but was made sweeter to appeal to Americans.

A little sweet with easy, one-step breaded chicken, this dish comes together quickly and can hit the table in 30 minutes. I intentionally chose a fast breading method to save time, but if you want a thicker, crispier breading, use the breading from my Crispy Honey Garlic Chicken (page 79); just note that the breading is not egg-free.

FOR THE CHICKEN:

½ cup arrowroot, potato, or cassava flour
1 teaspoon garlic salt
1 teaspoon ground black pepper
1 pound boneless, skinless chicken breasts, excess fat trimmed and cut into small pieces
¼ cup coconut oil or other high-heat oil

FOR THE SAUCE:

½ cup orange juice
¼ cup coconut aminos
¼ cup Date Paste (page 269)
1 tablespoon arrowroot flour
1 tablespoon minced fresh garlic
½ teaspoon crushed red pepper flakes (optional)

1 **MAKE THE CHICKEN:** In a medium bowl or large reusable bag, combine the flour, garlic salt, and pepper. Add the chicken and stir or shake until coated.

recipe continues

2 In a large saucepan, heat the oil over medium heat. Add the marinated chicken and cook until it's crispy and light brown, 5 to 6 minutes on each side. Transfer the chicken to a bowl or plate and set aside. Leave the pan on the stove to make the sauce.

3 **MAKE THE SAUCE:** In a small bowl, stir together the orange juice, coconut aminos, date paste, and flour. Set aside.

4 Drain all but 1 tablespoon of the oil from the same pan in which you cooked the chicken. Add the garlic and cook over medium heat until light brown, 1 to 2 minutes. Stir in the orange juice mixture and cook for 30 seconds to 1 minute, until it has thickened. Add the red pepper flakes (if using). Fold in the chicken breasts and serve.

Freeze in a sealed container for up to 3 months.

Bacon-Wrapped Ranch Chicken

WHOLE 30   

SERVES:	PREP TIME:	COOK TIME:
4	10 minutes	20 minutes

Pictured on page 94

Make It a Meal

We love this paired with my Roasted Potatoes (page 121) and Crispy Freezer Veggies (page 247) or Caesar Salad (page 204, sans chicken). And my boys love to dip this in my Homemade Ranch Dressing (page 251) for double ranch flavor.

Sometimes after a full day of work, I just don't want to make dinner. Simple recipes like this help dinner feel approachable. The chicken is seasoned with an easy rub and then wrapped in bacon to level up the flavor. Can't find Whole30-compatible bacon? You can make this chicken without the bacon under the broiler or in an air fryer or grill the chicken after the rub is added.

1 pound boneless, skinless chicken breasts, excess fat trimmed and meat cut into strips
2 tablespoons Ranch Seasoning (page 265)
1 pound sliced bacon
Toothpicks (optional)

1 **IF MAKING THESE IN THE OVEN:** Turn the oven to broil (high if you have an oven with the choice of high or low broil). Line a rimmed baking sheet with parchment paper. If you have one, set a cooling rack on your baking sheet, which will allow the bacon grease to drain and keep the bacon crispy. If not, cook the chicken directly on the parchment paper.

2 Sprinkle the chicken with the ranch seasoning and rub it all over. Wrap each piece of chicken with half a piece of bacon. (Optional: Secure the bacon with a toothpick [just be sure to take them out before eating!]) Try to avoid overlapping the bacon too much, as the overlapped bacon won't cook as well. Lay the wrapped chicken on the cooling rack (if using) or parchment-lined baking sheet.

3 Broil the chicken for 10 minutes then flip. If not using a cooling rack, carefully drain off the grease before you flip. Broil for another 10 minutes. The chicken is done when the bacon is crispy and the chicken is cooked through with no pink in the center.

Prep the chicken as described above. Air fry at 400°F for 7 minutes, flip or shake, and then cook for 7 minutes more, until the bacon is crispy.

Out-N-In Burger Bites

WHOLE 30  	SERVES: 4	PREP TIME: 20 minutes	COOK TIME: 15 minutes

Pictured on page 95

▸ **Note: I call for baking these in the oven, but you could cook them in a large saucepan over medium-high heat, though it takes a bit of hands-on work to make sure they're browned evenly on all sides. It's also more difficult to keep the balls of meat round. To make the burger bites egg-free, use a vegan mayo such as Primal Kitchen's Vegan Mayo. You can also find vegan mayo recipes online.**

◎ Make It a Meal

Delicious paired with my Onion Rings (page 212) or Whole30 Potato Salad (page 240) and Creamy Fruit Salad (page 234) or fruit.

You can't live in California without being aware of a very famous burger chain that only sells burgers and fries, and man are they good at what they do! My oldest son got his first job there, and all the youngers fell in love with their food and want to follow suit. Of course I had to re-create these favorite flavors at home. The burger bites are fun for dinner or they make a great appetizer. You can assemble your own burger bites with your toppings of choice—onion, tomato, lettuce, avocado, bacon—then dip them in the special sauce.

FOR THE SPECIAL SAUCE:

- ½ cup Homemade Mayo (page 253), or store-bought (see Note)
- 3 tablespoons ketchup
- 3 tablespoons Date Paste (page 269; only needed if using unsweetened ketchup)
- 1 tablespoon finely chopped pickle
- 1½ teaspoons white distilled vinegar
- ¼ teaspoon paprika
- ⅛ teaspoon salt

FOR THE BURGER BITES:

- 1 pound ground beef
- 1 teaspoon salt
- ½ teaspoon ground black pepper
- 28 toothpicks
- Toppings of choice, cut into bite-size pieces

1 **MAKE THE SAUCE:** In a small bowl, combine the mayo, ketchup, date paste (if using), pickle, vinegar, paprika, and salt. Mix well. Store in the fridge until ready to use. Extra sauce can be stored in the fridge for up to 2 weeks.

2 **MAKE THE BITES:** Preheat the oven to 400°F. Line a rimmed baking sheet with parchment paper and set a cooling rack inside, if you have one.

3 Shape the ground beef into about 28 (1-tablespoon) balls. Do your best to handle the meat as little as possible, which can make the burgers tougher. Arrange the balls on the cooling rack or parchment paper and sprinkle with the salt and pepper. Bake for 15 minutes, until no longer pink inside.

Cook burger bites in a single layer at 350°F for 10 minutes.

4 Serve the bites on toothpicks with the toppings along with the special sauce.

Corndog Muffins

		SERVES: 12	PREP TIME: 15 minutes	COOK TIME: 26 to 28 minutes

What kid doesn't love corndogs? But most of the store-bought versions have a looong list of ingredients, and homemade alternatives can be a pain to hand-dip. These are easy, have the flavor of corndog batter plus hot dogs with simple ingredients, and freeze great. My boys prefer these with thinly sliced hot dogs so there is some hot dog in every bite.

Make It a Meal

Delicious paired with my Caulitots (page 219) or Carrot Fries (page 216) and Cobb Salad (page 206, sans chicken).

Freeze in a single layer, then store in a sealed container for up to 3 months.

½ cup coconut flour
½ cup tapioca flour
1 teaspoon salt
1 teaspoon baking powder
½ cup extra-light-tasting olive oil or coconut oil, melted and cooled
⅓ cup honey
4 large eggs
¾ cup full-fat coconut milk
8 hot dogs, cut into thin rounds

1 Preheat the oven to 350°F. Spray a muffin tin with cooking spray. If you prefer to use muffin liners, spray those with cooking spray to prevent sticking.

2 In a medium bowl, combine the flours, salt, and baking powder with a whisk or spatula.

3 Add the oil, honey, eggs, and coconut milk to the dry ingredients and whisk or stir until just combined.

4 Let the batter rest while you slice the hot dogs into thin circles. Add the hot dogs to the batter, stirring until just combined. Scoop the batter evenly into each prepared muffin cup, about ¼ cup each.

5 Cook for 26 to 28 minutes, until the top springs back when touched.

6 Serve warm. My boys love them served with ketchup or my Whole30 Date Mustard Sauce (page 250).

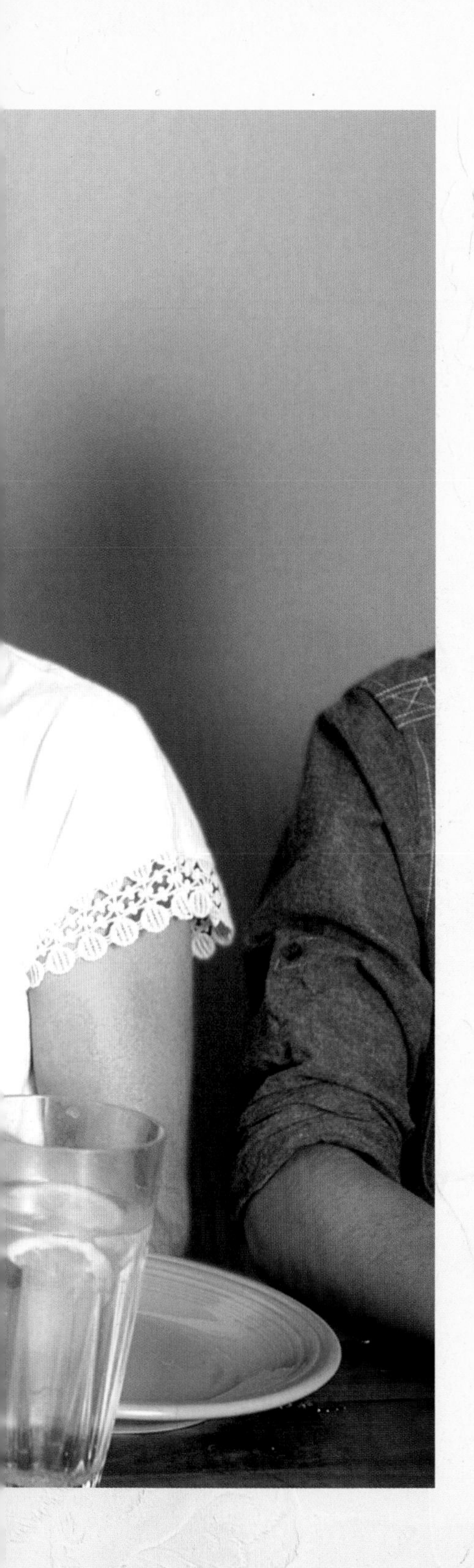

Classics with a Makeover

3 CHAPTER

Chicken-Fried Steak Bites

WHOLE 30   

SERVES:	PREP TIME:	COOK TIME:
6	20 minutes	20 to 25 minutes

Note: To make this egg-free, use 1 cup coconut milk total instead of the egg–coconut milk combination for the steak breading.

Make It a Meal

We love these paired with my Mashed Potatoes (page 105), Balsamic Brussels Sprouts (page 233) or steamed peas, and Cloud Drop Biscuits (page 223, not Whole30).

Growing up, we didn't go out to eat a lot. But when we did, one of my very favorite things to order, as a true Texas girl, was chicken-fried steak with white gravy and a chocolate milkshake. I was literally dancing around the kitchen when I finally got this recipe nailed down. It's easy to make these steak bites without a lot of intensive individual breading, and there's a secret ingredient that makes them crispy without using any nut flour. Plus, they turn out excellent whether cooked on the stove or in the air fryer.

FOR THE STEAK BITES:

1½ pounds cube steak
1 cup instant potato flakes
½ cup tapioca flour
1 teaspoon salt
½ teaspoon ground black pepper
½ teaspoon paprika
½ teaspoon garlic powder
¼ teaspoon onion powder
2 large eggs (see Note)
½ cup full-fat coconut milk
½ cup coconut or avocado oil, if using the stovetop
Cooking spray, if using an air fryer

FOR THE WHITE GRAVY:

1 cup full-fat canned coconut milk
3 tablespoons cassava flour
½ teaspoon salt
½ teaspoon ground black pepper
½ teaspoon onion powder

1 **MAKE THE BITES:** Sandwich the cube steaks in between two layers of paper towels. Lay a baking sheet, small pan, or large plate on top of them to help blot excess moisture. This will help the batter stick.

recipe continues

Chicken-Fried Steak Bites,
continued

2 In a food processor, combine the potato flakes, tapioca flour, salt, pepper, paprika, garlic powder, and onion powder. Pulse for 1 to 2 minutes, until the potato flakes have been ground more finely and the mixture is well blended. Transfer the mixture to a large reusable zip-top bag or bowl.

3 In a medium bowl, whisk together the eggs and the coconut milk.

4 Cut the steak into roughly 1-inch pieces. Toss the steak pieces in the dry ingredients to coat. Individually add the steak pieces to the egg-milk mixture, shaking off excess dry breading before adding, and toss until all the pieces are coated. Transfer the steak to a colander and let any excess coating drip off. Toss the steak in the dry ingredients once more until well breaded.

5 If cooking the steak on the stovetop, line a baking sheet with paper towels and set a metal cooling rack on top, if you have one. Using a cooling rack will help them maintain their crispiness. Set aside.

Lay the breaded steak in a single layer in the basket. Spray the steak pieces generously with cooking spray on all sides. Cook for 13 to 15 minutes, until crispy.

6 In a large saucepan, heat the oil over medium heat. Once the oil is hot, add the steak pieces in a single layer without crowding the pan. You will probably need to do this in two batches. Cook for about 4 minutes on each side, until the steak is golden and crispy. Transfer the cooked steak bites to the prepared baking sheet. Repeat with any remaining steak pieces.

7 **MAKE THE GRAVY:** While the steak is cooking, make the gravy. In a medium pot over medium heat, stir together the coconut milk, flour, salt, pepper, and onion powder. Cook for 1 to 2 minutes, stirring regularly, until the sauce thickens into a gravy. Watch closely because this happens quickly, and you don't want the gravy to get too thick. Remove the pot from the heat and serve the gravy with the steak bites.

Freeze the steak bites in a single layer on a cooling rack or baking sheet. Once frozen, store in a sealed container in the freezer for up to 3 months. Freeze the gravy separately from the steak bites.

Chicken or Turkey Mini Pot Pies

WHOLE 30 		SERVES: 4	PREP TIME: 15 to 30 minutes	COOK TIME: 40 minutes

Note: If you leave out the egg, the mashed potatoes on their own make a great Whole30-compatible mashed potato side dish.

This is my kind of comfort food. I love mashed potatoes, and using them as crust for these pies keeps them Whole30-compatible. I like making these into individual cups, but you could also skip those steps and cook this in a pie pan as a pot pie. Either way, the sauce makes a great gravy that you can use with any other chicken or turkey dish. You can also use whatever steamed veggies you like for this one. My kids prefer peas, carrots, and green beans. We love these paired with a green salad and my Creamy Fruit Salad (page 234).

FOR THE MASHED POTATOES:

- **1½ pounds white or gold potatoes, roughly chopped into cubes**
- **3 tablespoons Ghee (page 266), or store-bought**
- **3 tablespoons dairy-free milk of choice**
- **1 teaspoon salt**
- **1 large egg**

FOR THE GRAVY:

- **¼ cup plus 2 tablespoons Ghee (page 266), or store-bought**
- **¼ cup cassava flour**
- **1¼ cups chicken or turkey broth or bone broth**
- **2 teaspoons Flavor Boost Powder (page 258)**
- **½ teaspoon salt**

FOR THE FILLING:

- **1½ cups shredded chicken or turkey**
- **1 cup steamed or frozen veggies**

1 Preheat the oven to 425°F.

2 **MAKE THE POTATOES:** In a large pot, bring 10 cups of water to a boil over high heat, then add the potatoes. Boil until the

recipe continues

potatoes are tender, about 10 minutes. Drain the potatoes and return them to the pot. Add the ghee, milk, and salt and mash the potatoes until creamy. Stir in the egg until well combined.

3 If making individual pot pie cups, scoop 3 tablespoons of the mashed potato mixture into 12 muffin wells. Using the back of a spoon or another flat utensil that is slightly smaller than the muffin well, coat the inside of each well with the potatoes so that you've formed 12 pie "cups." Bake for 12 minutes until lightly browned. Do not turn off the oven. If making 1 large pie, set aside the mashed potatoes.

4 **MAKE THE GRAVY:** While the potatoes bake (or are set aside, if making a large pie), make the gravy. In a medium saucepan, melt the ghee over medium heat. Add the flour and stir until well combined, about 2 minutes. Stir in the broth, Flavor Boost Powder, and salt. Cook for 3 to 4 minutes more, until the mixture starts to thicken. Remove the pot from the heat and set aside.

5 **MAKE THE FILLING:** In a large bowl, combine the chicken or turkey and veggies. Stir in ¾ cup of the gravy. If making individual pot pie cups, add 2 generous tablespoons of filling to each mashed potato cup. Bake for 15 minutes, until mixture is bubbly and browned.

6 If making 1 large pie, add the filling to a 9-inch pie pan. Top with the mashed potatoes and bake for 30 minutes, just until potatoes begin to brown. Let cool for 10 minutes before serving.

7 Let the pies cool for 5 minutes before serving, then drizzle with the remaining gravy.

To freeze, store mini pot pies or remaining pot pie in a sealed container for up to 3 months.

Chicken Cordon Bleu,
continued

3 **MAKE THE CHEESE SAUCE:** In a small saucepan over medium heat, combine the coconut milk, tapioca flour, nutritional yeast, garlic powder, onion powder, and salt. Cook, stirring, until the mixture thickens and becomes tacky, 3 to 4 minutes. Remove the pot from the heat and allow the sauce to cool.

4 Lay a clean sheet of parchment paper on a work surface. Place one chicken half on the paper and top with 2 pieces of ham and 2 tablespoons of the cheese sauce. Roll up the chicken and secure it with a toothpick. Repeat with the remaining pieces of chicken.

5 In a small bowl, combine the starch, paprika, garlic salt, and pepper. In another small bowl, beat the eggs.

6 Carefully coat the chicken rolls first with the starch mixture, then with the egg, and then the starch mixture a second time. Shake off any excess after each step. Repeat with each chicken roll and arrange the dredged chicken on the prepared baking sheet. Spray them generously with cooking spray and bake for 30 minutes, until the chicken is cooked through and the outside is crispy.

Freeze in a sealed container for up to 3 months.

Salisbury Steak

WHOLE 30   

SERVES:	PREP TIME:	COOK TIME:
4	10 minutes	25 minutes

▾ **Note: Love mushrooms? You can also add 6 ounces of sliced fresh mushrooms to the gravy with the beef patties and simmer them for 10 minutes. Mushrooms are often traditionally served in this dish; our family just prefers it without.**

Make It a Meal

I recommend serving this dish with some Mashed Potatoes (page 105) and steamed peas with a side of Cloud Drop Biscuits (page 223, not Whole30).

This meal is comfort food at its easiest—it looks fancier than your typical weeknight meal and is filling without a lot of work behind it. While not essential to the recipe, the coconut aminos help boost the flavor.

FOR THE STEAK:

1 pound ground beef
1 tablespoon dried minced onion
1 tablespoon dried parsley
1 tablespoon coconut aminos (optional)
1 teaspoon garlic powder
1 teaspoon salt
1 teaspoon yellow mustard
2 tablespoons cassava flour
2 tablespoons coconut or avocado oil

FOR THE GRAVY:

1 cup beef broth or bone broth
½ tablespoon arrowroot flour
½ tablespoon coconut aminos (optional)
¼ teaspoon onion powder
¼ teaspoon salt
¼ teaspoon ground black pepper
½ small yellow onion, thinly sliced
Optional: ½ tablespoon Ghee (page 266), or store-bought

1 **MAKE THE STEAK:** In a medium bowl, combine the beef, onion, parsley, aminos (if using), garlic powder, salt, and mustard. I find this easiest to do with my hands. Divide the mixture evenly into 4 portions and shape each portion into a ½-inch-thick patty.

2 Place the 2 tablespoons of flour on a plate or shallow dish. Dredge each patty in the flour.

3 In a medium pan, heat the oil over medium heat. Once hot, add the patties and cook for 5 minutes on each side, until golden

recipe continues

brown. Remove the patties from the pan and set aside. Leave the pan on the stove for the gravy.

4 **MAKE THE GRAVY:** In a medium bowl, combine the broth, flour, aminos (if using), onion powder, salt, and pepper. Set aside.

5 In the same cooking pan, cook the onion over medium heat. If there isn't enough oil in the pan, add the ghee. Cook until the onion is translucent, about 5 minutes. Add the gravy mixture and cook until it starts to thicken, about 5 minutes more. Place the beef patties in the pan and simmer for 10 minutes, until the flavors combine.

Freeze in a sealed container for up to 3 months.

Easy Egg Rolls

WHOLE 30   	SERVES: 5*	PREP TIME: 30 minutes	COOK TIME: 15 minutes

*MAKES: 5 egg rolls

Note: An egg roll dipping sauce that doesn't have refined white sugar in it can be hard to find. My favorite sauce to use with these is my chilled Honey Garlic Glaze from the Crispy Honey Garlic Chicken recipe on page 79. For a Whole30 modification, eat just the filling on top of cooked cauliflower rice for a fast egg roll in a bowl. This Whole30 egg roll in a bowl is also delicious topped with the date-based Whole30 modification for the Honey Garlic Glaze (page 79).

Make It a Meal

We enjoy this paired with my Almond Green Bean Rice (page 230) and Creamy Fruit Salad (page 234).

Egg rolls have always intimidated me a little bit, so you can imagine how excited I was to re-create this delicious meal and with just five ingredients! Though egg rolls closely resemble the spring rolls of mainland China, their origin is somewhat disputed. Some say they are likely to have originated in Southern China, while others say it's part of the history of Chinese food in the US and was developed in the 1930s in New York.

Getting the egg roll wrapper right for Paleo was tricky, as traditional rolls have either rice or wheat in them. Coconut wraps (page 27), on the other hand, are a great swap because they're made from just coconut and are flexible enough to handle the rolling. Keep in mind that the coconut wraps won't get crispy like traditional egg roll wrappers do, but they'll still hold together nicely. This recipe makes 5 egg rolls, which we double for our large family.

2 cups thawed frozen stir-fry veggies
1 tablespoon olive or avocado oil, if using a less-fatty sausage like chicken or turkey
½ pound uncooked ground sausage of choice (pork, chicken, turkey)
½ cup Teriyaki Sauce (page 148)
5 coconut wraps
Dipping sauce of choice (see Note)

1 Preheat the oven to 350°F and line a baking sheet with parchment or foil. If you have a cooling rack, set one on the baking sheet to help the rolls get crisp on all sides.

recipe continues

2 In a food processor or with a knife, finely chop the thawed stir-fry veggies. In a large saucepan, heat the oil over medium heat. Add the sausage and chopped veggies and cook for 15 minutes, or until the sausage is cooked through and no longer pink. Remove the pan from the heat, drain any excess liquid, and stir in the teriyaki sauce until combined.

3 Lay a coconut wrap on a large piece of parchment with one point of the square wrap pointing toward you (it should look like a diamond). Scoop ⅓ cup of the filling mixture onto the coconut wrap, just above the bottom point.

4 To wrap, lift the bottom point of the wrap over the filling, then gently tuck it over the filling on the other side. Continue rolling toward the top point of the wrapper, folding in the sides and tucking them beneath the filling as you roll. Before you reach the top point, wet your finger with a little water and dab the top point to seal. Place the egg roll seam-side down on the prepared baking sheet.

Cook at 300°F for 12 minutes, rotating halfway through the cooking time.

5 Bake for 10 to 12 minutes, flipping halfway through the cooking time. The egg rolls should be browned and warmed through.

Freeze in a sealed container for up to 3 months.

Honey Orange-Glazed Ham

SERVES:	PREP TIME:	COOK TIME:
8	10 minutes	1½ hours

Ham is by far the favorite holiday meat in our house. My boys love when it's a little bit sweet, but I was not a fan of the ingredients and high sugar content of the glaze packets that usually come with the packaged hams. Then I realized how simple it is to make your own glaze. I added a fun twist with the orange flavor, but you can leave that out for a more traditional version. We like the flavor profile with half honey and half maple syrup, but you can use all of one or the other if you prefer.

1 (6-pound) spiral-cut ham
¼ cup honey
¼ cup pure maple syrup
2 tablespoons Ghee (page 266), or store-bought, melted
Zest of 1 large orange
Juice of 1 large orange (about ¼ cup)

1 Preheat the oven to 275°F and heat the ham per the package instructions. It's typically 15 minutes per pound, which is 1½ hours for a 6-pound ham. I like to keep the ham covered loosely with foil during this cook time.

2 **WHEN THE HAM HAS ABOUT 40 MINUTES LEFT, MAKE THE GLAZE:** In a medium bowl, combine the honey, maple syrup, ghee, orange zest, and orange juice. Generously brush the top of the ham with the glaze, trying to get down into all the cut crevices of the ham.

3 Cook uncovered for the last 40 minutes, brushing with the glaze every 10 minutes.

Freeze leftover ham in a sealed container for up to 3 months.

Garlic Steak Bites

WHOLE 30					SERVES: 8	PREP TIME: 10 minutes	COOK TIME: 15 minutes

Make It a Meal

We love this with a side of my Mashed Potatoes (page 105, sans egg), Crispy Freezer Veggies (page 247) like broccoli or green beans, and Cloud Drop Biscuits (page 223, not Whole30).

I looove air fried steak—crispy on the outside and still juicy on the inside. Toss the cubed steak with 3 tablespoons melted ghee and garlic salt. Air fry for 6 minutes at 350°F. Increase the heat to 400°F and cook for 2 to 5 minutes more, depending on your desired doneness. While the steak cooks, in a medium saucepan over medium heat, combine the ghee, fresh garlic, and garlic powder. Cook until the ghee is melted and the garlic is fragrant and lightly browned. When the steak is done, toss it with the ghee mixture.

Steak is my fancy dinner of choice. If I'm going to splurge on a nice Valentine's Day or birthday dinner, you bet it's going to be steak. Garlic steak is hands-down my favorite way to eat steak; the more garlic butter, the better! I fell in love with it in college when a friend's parents took us starving students to a fancy steak house. Best news: It's tremendously easy and doesn't even require you to fire up the grill.

1½ pounds top sirloin steak, cut into 1-inch cubes
5 tablespoons Ghee (page 266), melted, or store-bought
1 teaspoon garlic salt
2 tablespoons minced fresh garlic
1 teaspoon garlic powder

1. Let the meat rest at room temperature for 10 minutes before cooking.

2. **IF USING THE STOVE:** In a large skillet, melt 3 tablespoons of ghee over medium-high heat. Once hot, add the steak cubes in a single layer and sprinkle them with garlic salt. Cook until brown on all sides, 3 to 4 minutes.

3. Remove the steak from the pan. Reduce the heat to medium and add 2 tablespoons ghee, fresh garlic, and garlic powder. Cook for 2 to 3 minutes, until the ghee is melted and the garlic is fragrant and lightly browned. Return the steak to the pan and cook 2 to 3 minutes or until preferred doneness, tossing it in the ghee and garlic.

Freeze in a sealed container for up to 3 months.

Potatoes and Sausage Gravy

WHOLE 30  

SERVES:	PREP TIME:	COOK TIME:
4	10 minutes	30 minutes

I grew up in Houston, Texas, and do they ever know comfort food. Biscuits and gravy are a well-known Southern comfort food dish, and this is a Whole30-compatible twist on it that still checks all the boxes. This is also my go-to recipe for roasted potatoes that are simple but tasty. We eat them at least once a week.

FOR THE ROASTED POTATOES:

1 pound white or yellow potatoes, cut into small wedges
1 tablespoon extra-virgin olive or avocado oil
1 teaspoon salt
½ teaspoon paprika

FOR THE SAUSAGE GRAVY:

1 batch uncooked Homemade Breakfast Sausage (page 57) or 1 pound ground breakfast sausage
2½ cups full-fat coconut milk
¼ cup cassava flour
¼ teaspoon salt
¼ teaspoon ground black pepper

1 **MAKE THE POTATOES:** Preheat the oven to 425°F. Line a baking sheet with parchment paper and set aside.

2 On the prepared baking sheet, toss the potato wedges with the olive oil, salt, and paprika until well coated. Make sure they're evenly spread over the baking sheet and roast for 30 minutes, until browned and tender.

3 **MAKE THE GRAVY:** While the potatoes are roasting, in a large saucepan, cook the sausage over medium heat. In a medium bowl, whisk together the coconut milk, flour, salt, and pepper. Add to the sausage when it is no longer pink in the center. Cook until the gravy thickens, stirring constantly, for 2 to 3 minutes. Reduce the heat to low until the potatoes are ready. Serve the gravy over the roasted potatoes.

Note: Instead of using coconut milk and cassava flour for the gravy, you can use 3 cups of steamed cauliflower plus 1 cup coconut milk plus the salt and pepper, pureed until smooth and then cooked as described in the recipe. That's my veggie hack for this recipe!

Make It a Meal

The sausage gravy is also delicious on top of my Mashed Potatoes (page 105) or my Cloud Drop Biscuits (page 223, not Whole30), with a side of Crispy Freezer Veggies (page 247) like broccoli.

Whole30 Lasagna

WHOLE 30  

SERVES:	PREP TIME:	COOK TIME:
6	30 minutes	1¼ hours

Note: This will make a 9 x 9-inch pan of lasagna, but you can increase the recipe 1½ times if you want to make a large 9 x 13-inch pan. I prefer the ground meat to be half pork, half beef, but you can use all of one or the other. Prep time will depend on whether you buy or make your marinara sauce, ricotta, and dairy-free mozzarella. If you have access to store-bought dairy-free ricotta, dairy-free mozzarella (instead of the mozzarella sauce), and marinara, that will make the prep much simpler. If you go the store-bought route, use 1 cup dairy-free ricotta and 1½ cups dairy-free mozzarella.

I'm not a big pasta person, but lasagna gets me every time. I love all the layers and flavors. I was thrilled when I came up with this Whole30-compatible version using thin slices of white sweet potatoes that taste almost like lasagna noodles. My kids literally said, "These *noodles* taste good." The key is to get the slices nice and thin, which I do with a mandoline slicer.

FOR THE DAIRY-FREE ALMOND RICOTTA CHEESE:

- 1½ cups slivered or sliced almonds
- 3 tablespoons nutritional yeast
- 1½ teaspoons dried basil
- 1 teaspoon salt or garlic salt
- ½ cup water
- 1 large egg (optional)

FOR THE DAIRY-FREE MOZZARELLA SAUCE:

- 1½ cups full-fat coconut milk
- 3 tablespoons tapioca starch
- ¼ cup nutritional yeast
- ½ teaspoon garlic powder
- ½ teaspoon onion powder
- ½ teaspoon salt

FOR THE LASAGNA:

- 1½ cups ground meat of choice (see Note)
- 1 teaspoon salt
- ½ teaspoon ground black pepper
- 4 cups (32 ounces) Pantry Marinara Sauce (page 268), or store-bought
- 2 large white sweet potatoes, sliced lengthwise into very thin strips

Make It a Meal

We love this with Caesar Salad (page 204, sans chicken), fruit, and my Paleo Breadsticks (page 237, not Whole30).

1 **MAKE THE ALMOND RICOTTA:** In a blender or food processor, combine the almonds, nutritional yeast, basil, and salt with ½ cup water and blend until smooth. Pause to scrape down the sides of the blender or food processor as needed. Stir in the egg (if using). This will make the ricotta easier to spread. Set aside.

2 **MAKE THE MOZZARELLA SAUCE:** In a blender, combine the coconut milk, tapioca starch, nutritional yeast, garlic powder, onion powder, and salt and blend until smooth. Transfer the mixture to a medium saucepan and cook over medium heat until it thickens, stirring regularly, about 5 minutes. Set aside.

3 **MAKE THE LASAGNA:** Preheat the oven to 400°F.

4 In a large saucepan over medium heat, cook the ground meat with a sprinkle of the salt and pepper until the meat is no longer pink, 10 minutes.

5 If making my Pantry Marinara Sauce for this recipe, combine all the ingredients with the meat in the pan while it simmers. Otherwise, add the store-bought sauce to the pot when the meat is done cooking.

6 **TO ASSEMBLE:**

LAYER ONE: Pour 1 cup of the marinara and meat sauce into the bottom of a 9 x 9-inch pan and spread to coat. Top with one layer of thinly sliced potato, laying the slices side by side vertically. Top with one-third of the ricotta mixture, 1 cup of the marinara sauce, and one-third of the cheese sauce.

LAYER TWO: Lay down another layer of potatoes, this time horizontally. Top with one-third of the ricotta mixture, another cup of marinara sauce, and one-third of the cheese sauce.

LAYER THREE: Add another layer of potatoes, going vertically. Top with the final one-third of the ricotta mixture and another cup of marinara sauce.

recipe continues

Whole30 Lasagna,
continued

LAYER FOUR: Add the last layer of potatoes horizontally and top them with the last cup of marinara sauce. Drizzle with the remaining cheese sauce.

7 Cover the pan with foil that has been sprayed with cooking oil on the side touching the top of the lasagna so the cheese won't stick. Cook, covered, for 65 minutes. Remove the foil and cook for 10 minutes more, until the sauce is bubbly and the top is golden.

Freeze cooked lasagna in single servings in sealed containers for up to 3 months.

Enchilada Dip Bake

WHOLE 30  

SERVES:	PREP TIME:	COOK TIME:
8	15 minutes	35 minutes

There's a lot that I love about this dish. I can throw it together quickly and easily, and it makes a 9 x 13-inch pan, big enough to feed the entire family. I steam my chicken in the Instant Pot and then shred it using my hand mixer or standing mixer. Make-ahead tip: I always prep extra steamed, shredded chicken and then freeze it for when I need it.

Make It a Meal

We love to use Tostones (page 224) for scooping, but it's also delicious on some cauliflower rice, and we pair it with my Cilantro Salsa Slaw (page 243) and fruit.

1 (13-ounce) can chilled coconut cream, solid part only (see directions)
1 (16-ounce) jar salsa verde
¼ cup nutritional yeast
1 teaspoon garlic salt
5 cups cooked and shredded chicken (about 1½ pounds)
½ to 1 cup dairy-free cheddar cheese (optional)
Optional: 1 batch Tostones (page 224) or other gluten-free chip of choice, for serving

1 Preheat the oven to 350°F.

2 Open the can of chilled coconut cream. Drain and set aside the cloudy liquid (you can use this in smoothies or just toss it), reserving the solid white coconut cream.

3 In a blender or food processor, combine the coconut cream, salsa, nutritional yeast, and garlic salt and blend until creamy. Fold in the chicken.

4 Spread the chicken mixture over the bottom of a 9 x 13-inch pan and sprinkle with cheese (if using). Bake for 30 minutes, or until the mixture is bubbling around the edges. Turn the oven to Broil and continue cooking until the top of the casserole browns. Once brown, remove the pan from the oven and let it cool for 10 to 15 minutes. The sauce will thicken as it cools.

5 While the enchilada dip bakes, prepare the tostones (if using). Serve the dip with the tostones or chips, if desired.

Meals in a Snap (30 Minutes or Less)

CHAPTER 4

Italian Toss & Bake Chicken

WHOLE 30

SERVES:	PREP TIME:	COOK TIME:
4	10 minutes	20 minutes

Make It a Meal

It's great with my Pantry Marinara Sauce (page 268), zoodles or other spiralized veggie, or cauliflower gnocchi (not Whole30), my Caesar Salad (page 204, sans chicken) and Paleo Breadsticks (page 237, not Whole30).

Freeze in a single layer on a baking pan or cooling rack. Once frozen, store together in a sealed container for up to 3 months.

Spray chicken strips generously with cooking oil spray and air fry at 350°F for 12 to 15 minutes, until the chicken is golden and cooked through. The cooking time will depend on the size of your strips, the size of your air fryer, and how full you load the basket.

As a child of the nineties, I 100 percent remember the classic boxed chicken seasoning that promised you could just shake the topping onto the chicken and then bake without a lot of fussy coating steps. This toss-and-bake recipe brings that simplicity back without the additives of processed foods. The chicken is perfect for those evenings when you need something easy and fast. You can make this in the oven or in an air fryer.

⅔ cup almond flour
1½ teaspoons Italian seasoning
1 teaspoon salt
1 teaspoon paprika
½ teaspoon garlic powder
½ teaspoon onion powder
¼ teaspoon ground black pepper
1 pound boneless, skinless chicken breasts, cut into 1 x 2-inch strips
Cooking oil spray

1. If baking the chicken, preheat the oven to 350°F. Line a baking sheet with parchment paper and, if possible, set a metal cooling rack on top. Set aside.

2. In a medium bowl or large reusable zip-top bag, combine the flour, Italian seasoning, salt, paprika, garlic powder, onion powder, and pepper. Stir or shake to combine. Add the chicken pieces and toss or shake to coat. My littles love helping with this part—seal the reusable bag, put on some fun music, and have your kids shake their little hearts out!

3. If baking, lay the coated chicken on the metal rack or directly on top of the parchment paper. Spray generously with cooking oil spray. Cook for 20 minutes, until golden brown and cooked through, flipping halfway if not using the rack.

Creamy Jalapeño Chicken with Cilantro Lime Rice or Caulirice

WHOLE 30    

SERVES:	PREP TIME:	COOK TIME:
4	10 minutes	20 minutes

I love this simple but flavorful dish that comes together quickly. This is a meal that all my kids devour. I use only 2 chopped jalapeños in this to keep it milder for the young ones, but feel free to dial up the heat by using more! Two of my boys love spicy food, so I serve this with a dish of extra chopped jalapeños they can add on top.

FOR THE CREAMY JALAPEÑO CHICKEN:

1 cup full-fat canned coconut milk
2 tablespoons nutritional yeast
1 tablespoon arrowroot or potato starch
¾ teaspoon salt
2 to 4 jalapeños, seeded and finely chopped
1 tablespoon olive oil
1 pound boneless, skinless chicken breasts, cut into small pieces
¼ teaspoon ground black pepper

FOR THE CILANTRO LIME RICE OR CAULIRICE:

3 cups cooked or steamed white rice or cauliflower rice
2 tablespoons fresh lime juice
½ teaspoon salt
½ teaspoon onion powder
½ teaspoon garlic powder
1 cup packed fresh cilantro, chopped fine

1 **MAKE THE SAUCE:** In a medium bowl, whisk together the coconut milk, nutritional yeast, starch, and ½ teaspoon of the salt. Stir in the jalapeños. Set aside.

2 In a medium saucepan, heat the oil over medium heat. Add the chicken. Season with the remaining ¼ teaspoon salt and the pepper. Cook 6 to 7 minutes until the chicken is white but not cooked through. Add the sauce and cook for 7 to 8 minutes more, stirring occasionally, until the chicken is no longer pink inside and the sauce has thickened.

3 **MAKE THE RICE:** In a large bowl, combine the rice with the lime juice, salt, onion powder, and garlic powder. Stir well. Gently stir in the cilantro.

4 Serve the chicken over the rice.

Freeze rice and chicken together in a sealed container for up to 3 months.

BBQ Chicken Hash

WHOLE 30

SERVES:	PREP TIME:	COOK TIME:
4	5 minutes	25 minutes

My boys love BBQ chicken, and this hash is excellent for a fast meal or hearty breakfast. I love leaning on frozen veggies to help this dish come together quickly on a busy night. You can also use 4 cups frozen store-bought cubed hash browns to make this dish even faster!

2 tablespoons extra-virgin olive oil
1 pound boneless, skinless chicken breasts, chopped into 1-inch chunks
1 (16-ounce) bag frozen peppers and onions (often referred to as a "fajita mix")
1 cup Whole30 BBQ Sauce (page 256) or store-bought barbecue sauce
1 teaspoon garlic powder
1 teaspoon salt
4 cups steamed cubed russet or sweet potatoes
Optional: 1 cup fresh cilantro, chopped fine, for serving

1 In a large saucepan, heat the oil over medium-high heat. Add the chicken and frozen peppers and onions. Cook for 10 minutes, until the chicken is lightly browned and the veggies are tender.

2 As the chicken and veggies cook, combine the barbecue sauce, garlic powder, and salt with ¼ cup water in a medium bowl. Stir well. Pour the sauce over the chicken mixture and stir in the potatoes. Bring the mixture to a boil and reduce to a simmer. Cook for 15 minutes, or until the chicken is cooked through and the potatoes are tender. Top with the cilantro, if desired, and serve.

Freeze in a sealed container for up to 3 months.

Pineapple Chicken or Turkey Meatballs

WHOLE 30					SERVES: 20*	PREP TIME: 10 minutes	COOK TIME: 20 minutes

*MAKES: 20 meatballs

Meatballs are a great family-friendly and party-friendly food. This version was inspired by an Instagram live with Melissa Urban. Someone asked how to get better at creating recipes. She said it's helpful if you learn flavor combinations that go together well, such as chicken and pineapple. My boys love both, so I knew it was a flavor profile I needed to play around with. My boys said these tasted just like the ones they loved from the store but without gluten or added sugar.

Make It a Meal

I love serving these with fruit and a side of my Almond Green Bean Rice (page 230).

FOR THE MEATBALLS:

- **1 pound ground chicken or turkey**
- **½ cup canned crushed pineapple, drained and juices reserved**
- **½ teaspoon salt**
- **½ teaspoon paprika**
- **½ teaspoon onion powder**
- **½ teaspoon garlic powder**
- **2 tablespoons coconut or avocado oil, if using stovetop method**

FOR THE SAUCE:

- **2 teaspoons extra-virgin olive oil**
- **1 tablespoon minced fresh garlic**
- **1 cup pineapple juice, reserved from canned crushed pineapple**
- **¼ cup coconut aminos**

1. If using the oven method, preheat oven to 400°F. Line a baking sheet with parchment paper and a cooling rack, if you have one.

2. **MAKE THE MEATBALLS:** In a medium bowl, combine the ground meat, pineapple, salt, paprika, onion powder, and garlic powder. Mix until well incorporated.

3. Shape the meat mixture into 1½-tablespoon balls.

4. If cooking the meatballs in the oven, place the shaped meatballs on the cooling rack or parchment paper. Bake for 25 minutes, or until browned and no longer pink in the center.

Lay the meatballs in a single layer in the basket. Cook for 15 minutes at 350°F, or until they are cooked through with no pink in the center.

Freeze in a single layer on a cooling rack or baking sheet lined with parchment. Once frozen, store in the freezer in a sealed container for up to 3 months.

If cooking the meatballs on the stovetop, in a large saucepan, melt the coconut or avocado oil over medium heat. Place as many meatballs as will comfortably fit into the pan, making sure each has some space around it. Cook until the meatballs are browned on all sides and are no longer pink in the center, about 15 minutes.

5 **WHILE THE MEATBALLS ARE COOKING, MAKE THE SAUCE:** In a medium pot, heat the olive oil over medium heat. Add the garlic and cook until fragrant, 2 to 3 minutes. Stir in the pineapple juice and coconut aminos. Increase the heat, bring the mixture to a boil, and reduce to a simmer. Cook for 20 minutes, or until the liquid has reduced to ½ cup.

6 When the meatballs are done, toss them with the sauce and serve.

One-Pan Taco Rice

WHOLE 30					SERVES: 4	PREP TIME: 5 minutes	COOK TIME: 25 minutes

Make It a Meal

This is delicious on its own, but you could serve it on top of a bed of lettuce for extra greens, or serve it with my Tostones (page 224) for some crunch, topped with my Cilantro Lime Ranch (page 252). Also pairs well with my Cilantro Salsa Slaw (page 243).

Freeze in a sealed container for up to 3 months.

Sometimes you just need a fast and easy dinner, and this one-pan dish fits the bill! We love this with ground beef, but it will work with any ground meat of your choice. I love the convenience of using frozen veggies, but you can also cut up fresh bell peppers and onions, adding them at the same point in the recipe.

- 1 pound ground beef or meat of choice
- 1 (16-ounce) bag frozen peppers and onions (often referred to as a "fajita mix")
- 1 medium head fresh cauliflower, riced, or 1 (16-ounce) bag fresh or frozen riced cauliflower
- 1 (8-ounce) can tomato sauce
- 1 (10-ounce) can diced tomatoes with chiles, like Rotel
- 1 tablespoon chili powder
- 1 teaspoon ground cumin
- 1 teaspoon salt
- 1 cup fresh cilantro, finely chopped, for serving
- 1 cup Cilantro Lime Ranch (page 252), for serving
- Optional: Lettuce, Tostones (page 224), for serving

1. In a large skillet over medium heat, cook the ground beef, peppers and onions until the vegetables are tender and the beef is mostly cooked, about 10 minutes. Stir in the cauliflower, tomato sauce, tomatoes with chiles, chili powder, cumin, and salt. Bring the mixture to a boil then reduce to a simmer. Simmer for 10 minutes, or until most of the liquid has been absorbed.

2. When ready to serve, sprinkle the cilantro over the top and drizzle with the Cilantro Lime Ranch. Serve with lettuce or Tostones (page 224), if desired.

Sausage Green Bean Hash

WHOLE 30    

SERVES:	PREP TIME:	COOK TIME:
4 to 6	5 minutes	25 minutes

This easy skillet meal is wonderfully fast and still gets in two veggies and a protein. On a night I need dinner to come together quickly, this one is a winner. I love that it can be cooked on the stove or in the air fryer, and it's delicious by itself or with my Homemade Ranch Dressing (page 251). The red pepper flakes crank up the flavor and add a little kick that my family loves, and the ranch on top seals the deal.

¼ cup coconut or avocado oil
1½ pounds Yukon gold or red potatoes, chopped into 1-inch cubes
4 large (12-ounce) sausage links, sliced into ½-inch pieces
10 ounces frozen or fresh green beans
1½ teaspoons garlic salt
1 teaspoon paprika
1 teaspoon onion powder
1 teaspoon red pepper flakes (optional)
Optional: Homemade Ranch Dressing (page 251), for serving

1 In a large saucepan, heat the oil over medium heat. Add the potatoes in a single layer. Cook for 7 to 8 minutes, until the potatoes have browned on one side. Flip the potatoes and move them to one side of the pan. Add the sausage to the other side of the pan and the green beans on top of the potatoes and sausage. Sprinkle the mixture with the garlic salt, paprika, onion powder, and red pepper flakes (if using). Cover the pan with a lid and cook for 8 minutes more.

2 Remove the lid and stir. Cook, uncovered, for 5 to 6 minutes more, until the green beans are tender, the potatoes are crispy, and the sausage has browned. Serve topped with ranch, if desired.

In a medium bowl, combine the oil and chopped potatoes, stirring until all the potatoes are coated with oil. Air fry at 350°F for 8 minutes. Stir and add sliced sausage, green beans, and seasonings. Air fry for 8 to 10 minutes more, until potatoes are crispy and green beans are starting to crisp.

Freeze in a sealed container for up to 3 months.

Pesto Chicken Potato Skillet

WHOLE 30			SERVES: 4	PREP TIME: 15 minutes	COOK TIME: 15 minutes

Make It a Meal

I like serving this with my Cobb Salad (page 206, sans chicken), Cloud Drop Biscuits (page 223, not Whole30), and some fruit.

I love pesto. It's fantastic on noodles, chicken, or even in an omelet and it is so easy to make! This combination of pesto, chicken, and potatoes comes together quickly but tastes like you spent much longer than 30 minutes making it. It's one of my husband's favorite meals. I prefer the fresh flavor of homemade pesto, but you can also use a store-bought Whole30-compatible pesto to make this a quicker five-ingredient meal. I use cashews in my pesto to keep the cost down, but you can also use an equal amount of pine nuts.

FOR THE PESTO:

½ cup whole unsalted cashews
3 cups packed fresh basil
2 fresh garlic cloves, chopped
⅓ cup extra-virgin olive oil
Pinch of salt

FOR THE SKILLET:

2 tablespoons extra-virgin olive oil
1 pound boneless, skinless chicken breasts, cut into 1-inch pieces
1 pound white sweet potatoes or russet potatoes, spiralized
1 teaspoon salt or garlic salt

1 **MAKE THE PESTO:** In a food processor or blender, finely chop the cashews until they form a coarse meal. Add the basil, garlic, olive oil, and salt and blend until smooth. You may need to pause to scrape down the sides of the blender or food processor, then blend or process once again. Set aside.

2 **MAKE THE SKILLET:** In a large saucepan, heat the oil over medium heat. Add the chicken breast pieces. Cook for 5 minutes, until the chicken is white but not fully cooked. Add the spiralized potato on top of the chicken, cover, and steam for 6 to 7 minutes, until the potatoes are just tender. Stir in the pesto and cook, uncovered, for 2 minutes more to warm through. Season with the salt and serve.

Taco Tuna Fritters

WHOLE 30   	SERVES: 4	PREP TIME: 5 minutes	COOK TIME: 20 minutes

Make It a Meal

We enjoy these with my Cilantro Salsa Slaw (page 243) and Creamy Fruit Salad (page 234).

Canned tuna can be hard to love. I wouldn't touch the stuff until I was at least twenty years old, and that was because we were poor college students and it was what we could afford. This dish makes tuna tasty again with taco seasoning and the crispiness of a fritter. The first time I made these, my pickiest eater devoured them and asked for more with no clue he'd just eaten tuna, a food he had never tried before! A great sauce is the clincher for these—I love them with Cilantro Lime Ranch (page 252), and my hubby prefers my Chipotle Mayo (page 253).

1½ cups shredded sweet potato (from 1 medium potato)
1 (5-ounce) can light tuna packed in water, drained
2 large eggs
¼ cup tapioca or arrowroot flour
1 batch Taco Seasoning Mix (page 255) or 2½ tablespoons store-bought
¼ cup coconut or avocado oil
Optional: Cilantro Lime Ranch (page 252) or Chipotle Mayo (page 253), for serving

1. In a medium bowl, combine the sweet potato, tuna, eggs, flour, and Taco Seasoning Mix. Mix until thoroughly incorporated.

2. In a medium saucepan, heat the oil over medium heat. When the oil is hot, add 2 tablespoons of the tuna mixture to the oil, flattening the middle of the fritter to help it cook evenly. Repeat with 2 to 3 more fritter scoops, depending on your pan size. Cook for 3 to 4 minutes on each side, until the fritters are crispy. Repeat with the remaining tuna mixture.

3. Serve with Cilantro Lime Ranch or Chipotle Mayo, if desired.

Freeze the fritters in a single layer until frozen, then store in a sealed bag or container for up to 3 months.

BBQ Chicken

WHOLE 30					SERVES: 4	PREP TIME: 5 minutes	COOK TIME: Varies*

*COOK TIME VARIES BY METHOD: 15 minutes in Instant Pot, 25 to 30 minutes in oven, 3 hours on high or 6 hours on low in slow cooker

Make It a Meal

This is delicious served on top of my Roasted Potatoes (page 121) or sweet potatoes, cubed or whole, tater tots (not Whole30), or my Caulitots (page 219)! Another easy option is to serve it on gluten-free buns (not Whole30). Pair with my Whole30 Potato Salad (page 240) and Caesar Salad (page 204, sans chicken).

This two-ingredient chicken dish is a wonderfully easy answer to dinner in a flash. It's simple but with so many variations and ways to enjoy it, you will find yourself going to this again and again. I love that it can be made in the Instant Pot, oven, or slow cooker, depending on what you have on hand. Using my easy Whole30 BBQ Sauce (page 256) makes this budget-friendly too!

1 pound boneless, skinless chicken breasts, excess fat trimmed

1 cup Whole30 BBQ Sauce (page 256) or store-bought

1. **IF USING AN INSTANT POT:** Place the chicken breasts in the Instant Pot and cover them completely with the sauce. Seal and cook on Manual for 15 minutes.

   IF USING THE OVEN: Place the chicken breasts in a 9 x 9-inch pan and cover them completely with the sauce. Bake at 350°F for 25 to 30 minutes, or until no longer pink in the center.

   IF USING A SLOW COOKER: Place trimmed chicken breasts in the bottom of your slow cooker. Top with BBQ sauce. Cover and cook on low for 6 hours or high for 3 hours, until chicken is tender and easy to shred and no longer pink in the center.

2. Once the chicken is cooked, remove it from the sauce and shred. See page 195 for my tips on shredding chicken. Return the shredded chicken to the sauce and stir to combine.

Store in a sealed container in the freezer for up to 3 months.

BBQ Chicken Quesadillas (not Whole30)

In a skillet or pan on medium heat, layer 1 Cassava Flour Tortilla (page 244) with 3 tablespoons dairy-free shredded cheese, ⅓ cup shredded BBQ Chicken, another 3 tablespoons cheese, topped with 1 more tortilla. Cook for 3 to 4 minutes, flip, and then cook 3 to 4 minutes more, until tortilla is crunchy and cheese is melted. These are delicious dipped in Ranch (page 251).

BBQ Chicken Salad (Whole30)

Use this instead of plain roasted chicken in the Cobb Salad (page 206), and serve it with Date Mustard (page 250) or Ranch (page 251).

Chicken or Beef Stir-Fry with Teriyaki Sauce

WHOLE 30    

SERVES:	PREP TIME:	COOK TIME:
4	10 minutes	20 minutes

Stir-fry is a fast dinner option that's loaded with veggies. It is based on a Chinese cooking technique of cooking ingredients in a small amount of hot oil while being stirred in a wok. Though the teriyaki cooking technique is believed to have come from seventeenth-century Japan, teriyaki sauce is thought to have originated in Hawaii with the arrival of the first Japanese immigrants, who invented a new marinade mixing local products like pineapple juice with soy sauce, which eventually became the teriyaki sauce we know today. Whole30-compatible teriyaki sauce can be expensive or hard to find, so this recipe includes an easy homemade sauce. I love the texture of adding the crushed cashews. With its minimal ingredients, veggies you can grab from the freezer, and quick cook time, don't be surprised if you make this one on the regular!

FOR THE TERIYAKI SAUCE:

⅓ cup coconut aminos
¼ cup balsamic vinegar
¼ cup orange juice
2 tablespoons Date Paste (page 269)
1 tablespoon potato or arrowroot starch
1 teaspoon salt
½ teaspoon ground ginger
½ teaspoon garlic powder

FOR THE STIR-FRY:

1 tablespoon cooking oil, such as olive, avocado, or sesame
1 pound boneless, skinless chicken breasts or flank steak, cut into small pieces
½ teaspoon salt
¼ teaspoon ground black pepper
1 (12-ounce) bag frozen stir-fry veggies
Cooked rice or cauliflower rice, for serving
Optional: 2 tablespoons sesame seeds, ¼ cup crushed salted cashews, for topping

1 **MAKE THE SAUCE:** In a medium bowl, whisk together the coconut aminos, vinegar, juice, date paste, starch, salt, ginger, and garlic powder. Set aside.

2 **MAKE THE STIR-FRY:** In a large saucepan, heat the oil over medium-high heat. Add the chicken or beef. Season with salt and pepper and cook until the meat is no longer pink. Add the frozen veggies and cook for 2 minutes, until they start to soften. Stir in the teriyaki sauce and cook until the veggies are tender and the sauce thickens, about 5 minutes. If the sauce is still too thin, mix 1 tablespoon of starch with 1 tablespoon of water to create a slurry. Stir the slurry into the pan and cook until the sauce thickens, 1 to 2 minutes.

Freeze with rice in a sealed container for up to 3 months.

3 Serve over the cauliflower rice or cooked rice (not Whole30) and top with the sesame seeds and cashews, if desired.

Lunch Box 101

5 CHAPTER

Stuck on What to Pack for Lunch?

Whether for your kids or yourself, meals outside the home can be overwhelming. That was one of the first things my boys and I tackled when we switched to eating Paleo. We created a list of lunch box options so they (read: *I*) would feel empowered instead of overwhelmed about what to pack for lunch.

My boys pack their own lunches, so here is how we approached it: I encouraged them to make sure every lunch had a protein, healthy fat, and fruit or veggie. I taught them proteins are like the Legos of the body—we need them to build strong muscles, tissues, and organs; that healthy fats are superheroes for helping us stay full; and that fruits and veggies have fiber and vitamins to keep us healthy. All of my lunch box examples are built around that basic formula—a protein, healthy fat (nuts, seeds, oil-based dipping sauce like ranch), plus fruits and veggies, with a sprinkling of fun sides like pudding, gelatin, vanilla wafers, or muffins. But even those fun sides are full of nutrient-dense whole food ingredients (shhh!).

And guess what? I also build my lunch around a similar formula—it's not just for kids! From Whole30, I learned to base my meals on one or two palm-sized servings of protein, a plate full of veggies, healthy fat, and fruit, if desired. Building my plate this way has made a *huge* difference in my satiety and cravings.

This lunch box section was a labor of love—my boys now feel that they have more options eating Paleo for lunches than our old PB&J days. I hope these boxes inspire you and give you a new collection of lunchtime favorites that you can mix and match!

Blueberry Muffin (page 161)

Our Favorite Chicken Strips (page 70)

Paleo Vanilla Wafers (page 178)

Lemon Poppyseed Muffin (page 161)

Hummus and Plantain Chips (page 164)

Kale Chips, meat stick or jerky

Cassava Flour Tortilla (page 244) Chocolate Nut Butter (page 262) and banana wraps

Vanilla Granola (page 38)

Bold Roasted Snack Mix (page 187)

Ham Rolls (page 167)

Chewy Chocolate Chip Granola Bars (page 157)

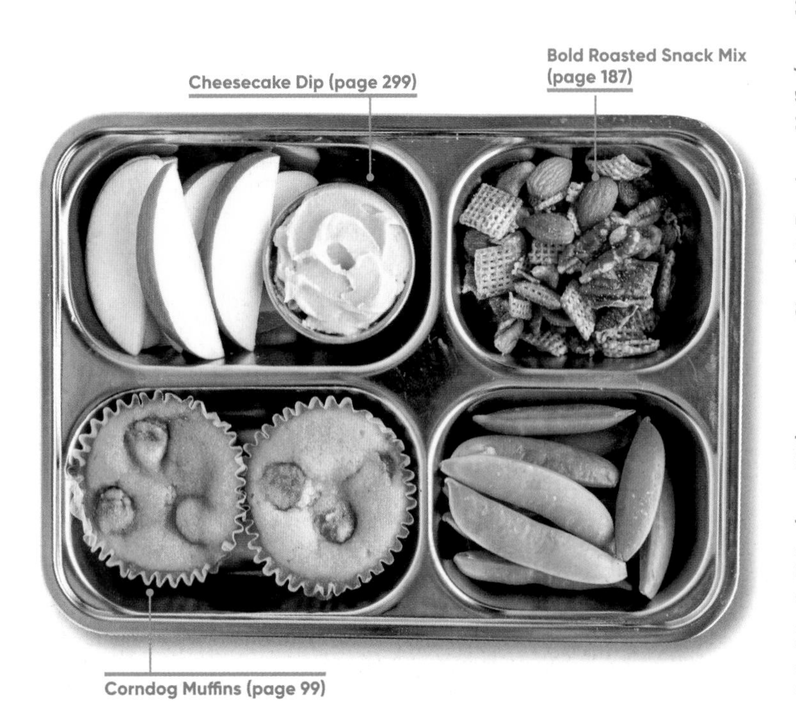

Tostones (page 224)
Chocolate Raspberry Muffin (page 161)
Baked Apple Chips (page 184)
Chicken Avocado Salad (page 170)

Tropical Twist DIY Trail Mix (page 172)
Protein Peanut Butter Bites (page 158)
Tuna Salad made with Date Mustard (page 250)

Chocolate Paleo Pudding (page 181)
Homemade Ranch Dressing (page 251)
Crispy Paleo Waffle with PB&J (page 49)

Chocolate Chip Muffin (page 161)
Fruit Juice Gelatin (page 183)
Classic DIY Trail Mix (page 172)

Ranch Roasted Snack Mix (page 187)
Egg Salad made with Date Mustard (page 250)
Protein Chocolate Chip Cookie Dough Bites (page 158)

Chewy Chocolate Chip Granola Bars

SERVES:	PREP TIME:	COOK TIME:
12*	15 minutes	25 minutes

*MAKES: 12 bars

Granola bars are such easy, tasty snacks and lunch box staples, but they often have a long list of ingredients including a lot of sugar. I'm thrilled to share these chewy, delicious bars that are a huge hit with my boys and have only seven ingredients! We usually make a double batch, baking in a 9 x 13-inch pan for 45 minutes.

Note: Make sure you use quick-cooking oats for these, not old-fashioned. Can't find mini chocolate chips? You can use regular chocolate chips chopped into fine pieces by hand or in a food processor. You can use pure maple syrup instead of honey, but since it is thinner, it will sink to the bottom of the granola bars a bit.

Freeze in an airtight container for up to 6 months.

¼ cup extra-light-tasting olive oil or coconut oil
½ cup honey
½ teaspoon salt
1 teaspoon vanilla extract
1¼ cups quick-cooking oats
1 cup crispy rice cereal
¼ cup dairy-free mini chocolate chips

1 Preheat the oven to 300°F.

2 In a medium saucepan over medium heat, combine the oil, honey, and salt. Cook for 2 minutes, until combined and heated through. Remove the pan from the heat and add the vanilla and oats. Stir until combined. Let the mixture sit for 5 minutes while you prepare the pan. Line a 9 x 9-inch baking pan with parchment paper.

3 Stir the crisp rice into the oat mixture. Sprinkle half of the chocolate chips over the parchment paper in the bottom of the pan. Spread the oat mixture over the top and sprinkle with the remaining 2 tablespoons chocolate chips. Top with a piece of parchment paper and press down, pressing the chocolate chips into the bars as well as evening them.

4 Bake for 30 minutes, until the bars are light brown around the edges. Let the bars cool completely in the pan before portioning them. Store in the pantry in an airtight container for up to a week.

Protein Cookie Dough Bites

SERVES:	PREP TIME:	COOK TIME:
20*	15 minutes	0 minutes

*MAKES: 20 cookie dough bites

These are such an easy grab-and-go snack or lunch box add-on. I love that they provide a good dose of protein and healthy fat but taste like cookie dough. They hold their shape at room temperature, but I recommend freezing them if you're traveling with them or packing them up for school. Even my boys enjoy making these bites. All of these can be made nut-free except the Chocolate Chip Cookie Dough Bites.

PEANUT BUTTER BITES

¼ cup peanut butter
2 tablespoons honey
½ teaspoon vanilla extract
¼ cup collagen powder
2½ to 4 tablespoons coconut flour
Optional: Coatings such as finely chopped nuts, chocolate chips, shredded coconut, cocoa powder, powdered sugar, or sprinkles

CAKE BATTER BITES

¼ cup cashew butter or sun butter
2 tablespoons honey
1 tablespoon vanilla extract
¼ cup collagen powder
¼ cup coconut flour
2 tablespoons sprinkles
Optional: Coatings such as finely chopped nuts, chocolate chips, shredded coconut, cocoa powder, powdered sugar, or sprinkles

CHOCOLATE BROWNIE BITES

¼ cup almond or sun butter
2 tablespoons honey
1 teaspoon vanilla extract
¼ cup collagen powder
2½ tablespoons coconut flour
2 tablespoons cocoa powder
Optional: Coatings such as finely chopped nuts, chocolate chips, shredded coconut, cocoa powder, powdered sugar, or sprinkles

CHOCOLATE CHIP COOKIE DOUGH BITES

2 tablespoons melted coconut oil
2½ tablespoons honey
½ tablespoon vanilla extract
¾ cup almond flour
¼ cup collagen powder
⅛ teaspoon salt
2 tablespoons mini dairy-free chocolate chips

recipe continues

1 In a medium bowl, combine all the wet ingredients and stir until smooth. Add the dry ingredients and stir until well combined. If making the chocolate chip cookie dough bites, don't add the chocolate chips until the batter comes together. For the peanut butter bites, use 2½ tablespoons coconut flour if your peanut butter is thick and holds its shape or 4 tablespoons if it is drippier and thinner.

2 The dough might seem too dry at first, but keep at it, using your hands to mix if needed. The final result should have the consistency of play dough and should not be sticky.

3 Roll the dough into small balls, about 1 tablespoon each, and place on a small baking pan or plate lined with parchment. If making peanut butter, cake batter, or chocolate brownie bites, roll the balls in your coating of choice. My boys love really finely chopped chocolate chips (which I work down to a powder in my mini food processor) for the peanut butter bites and maple sugar for the cake batter bites. For the cookie dough bites, no coating is needed. I recommend scooping small amounts onto the parchment without rolling, as they will crumble a bit and don't hold their shape until chilled.

4 These can be stored at room temperature for up to 1 week, though we love them cold out of the fridge, where you can store them for up to 2 weeks. If you are traveling with these at all, I recommend freezing the balls.

Freeze in a single layer and then store in the freezer together in a sealed container for up to 3 months.

All-Purpose Paleo Muffins

		SERVES: 12*	PREP TIME: 25 minutes	COOK TIME: 20 to 22 minutes

*MAKES: 12 muffins

▸ **Note: You can substitute honey for the maple syrup, though it will make your muffins denser. Add 2 tablespoons more milk to the batter to compensate. You can use coconut milk or other nondairy milk instead of the almond milk, but I recommend using coconut milk from a carton and not a can because it has a smoother consistency. Lastly, for a nut-free option, you can use 1 cup cassava flour instead of the almond and tapioca flour.**

A lot of Paleo muffins don't have a very soft texture, but these are spot-on! I wanted this to be an all-purpose base that could be combined with a variety of add-ins to create endless options. We share our favorites, but go ahead and have fun with it to create some new favorites of your own.

Nonstick cooking spray
½ cup unsweetened almond milk
1½ teaspoons lemon juice or white vinegar
2 cups almond flour (see Note)
½ cup tapioca or arrowroot flour
1 teaspoon baking powder
¼ teaspoon salt
¼ cup extra-light olive or coconut oil, melted
¼ cup pure maple syrup
1 large egg
1 teaspoon vanilla extract
Add-ins of choice (see Variations, page 163)

1 Preheat the oven to 350°F. Prepare a muffin tin by lining the wells with 12 muffin liners or coating them with nonstick cooking spray.

2 In a small bowl, stir together the almond milk and lemon juice. Set aside. This creates a faux "buttermilk" that makes a big difference in the muffins' texture. Don't skip this step!

3 In a medium mixing bowl, stir together the almond flour, tapioca or arrowroot flour, baking powder, and salt.

4 In a small mixing bowl, whisk together the oil, syrup, egg, and vanilla. Add the wet ingredients and the almond milk–lemon juice mixture to the dry ingredients. Stir gently, just until combined (overmixing your muffins will make them flat and dense). Stir in any mix-ins of choice.

recipe continues

All-Purpose Paleo Muffins,
continued

5 Fill each prepared muffin cup two-thirds full with batter, about ¼ cup each.

6 Bake for 20 to 22 minutes, until the tops of the muffins spring back when gently pressed. Cool the muffins in the tin on a cooling rack for 5 minutes, then enjoy! Store leftover muffins in an airtight container on the counter for 3 to 4 days, in the fridge for 10 days, or in the freezer for up to 6 months.

VARIATIONS

Add into prepared batter unless otherwise noted:

Blueberry Muffins

Add ½ cup fresh blueberries. You can add in 1 tablespoon lemon zest as well. Pour batter into muffin tin and bake as above.

Chocolate Chip Muffins

Add ¼ cup mini chocolate chips. Pour batter into muffin tin and bake as above.

Chocolate Raspberry Muffins

Mix together ½ cup raspberry jam + 1 tablespoon water. Stir ½ cup chocolate chips or chunks into the muffin batter, then gently swirl in the jam mixture. Pour the batter into the muffin tin and bake as above.

Cinnamon Roll Muffins

In a small bowl, stir together ½ cup coconut sugar, 2 tablespoons melted coconut oil, and 1 tablespoon ground cinnamon. Scoop 1 heaping tablespoon of muffin batter into each prepared muffin cup. Sprinkle 1 teaspoon of the cinnamon topping on top followed by another heaping tablespoon of batter. Finish with 1 teaspoon more of cinnamon topping.

Lemon Poppy Seed

Add 2 tablespoons lemon zest, 2 tablespoons poppy seeds, and 1 teaspoon lemon extract. **Optional:** Drizzle finished muffins with my Sugar Cookie Frosting (page 283).

smooth and creamy. You can store the hummus in the fridge in a sealed container for up to 3 weeks.

4 **MAKE THE PLANTAIN CHIPS:** If using an oven, preheat the oven to 350°F. Line a baking sheet with parchment paper and set aside.

5 Using a knife or mandoline, thinly slice the plantains. (The mandoline is king for this!)

6 In a large bowl, toss the plantain slices with the oil until all are coated. Lay the plantains in a single layer on either the prepared baking sheet or an air fryer tray. Sprinkle with salt.

7 If baking, bake the plantains for 25 to 30 minutes, or until crisped through.

Air fry the plantains at 350°F in a single layer (you will need to do this in batches) for 12 to 15 minutes, or until crisped through and lightly browned.

Ham Rolls

		SERVES: 8	PREP TIME: 30 minutes	COOK TIME: 10 minutes

When I was a kid, my mom would sometimes make this delicious handheld snack called ham sticks. It was simple: just homemade dough wrapped around pieces of ham, but I loved them. These are equally simple but just as adored by my boys. They're a fabulous portable lunch or travel food and taste great warm or cold. They have hiked up mountains with us.

1 pound boneless ham steak or leftover cooked ham
Tapioca or potato starch, for dusting
1 recipe Paleo All-Purpose Dough (page 236)

1 Preheat the oven to 350°F. Line a baking sheet with parchment paper and set aside. Trim the ham as desired of excess fat or skin and then slice it into long, skinny pieces, about 3 inches long by ½ inch wide.

2 Dust the counter with the starch. Roll out the dough with a rolling pin until it's about ¼ inch thick.

3 Wrapping the dough around the ham doesn't need to be fancy. I don't cut the dough into squares, though you could. I prefer the faster method of laying a cut piece of ham on the dough about ½ inch from the edge, then lifting the edge of the dough and wrapping it around the ham until it's covered. Then I pull the wrapped ham away from the dough until it breaks away. Smooth out the dough wrapping by rolling it on the counter with the palm of your hand, removing any excess or adding a little more as needed. Make sure the dough covers the ham completely, but

recipe continues

try not to have any more dough than you need. Place the dough-wrapped ham on parchment paper. Repeat with all of the ham rolls.

4 If you have extra dough, use it to make a small pizza crust, breadsticks, or rolls (see page 236).

5 Cook the ham rolls for 10 minutes. The dough will not brown, but it should feel solid to the touch. Don't overcook these, or they will be dry. Let the sticks cool on the counter. Store in the fridge in a sealed container for up to 1 week.

Freeze cooked in a single layer on a cooling rack or baking sheet lined with parchment until frozen. Then store together in the freezer in a sealed container for up to 3 months.

VARIATIONS

These are also delicious with shredded or sliced dairy-free cheddar cheese in addition to the ham. Also, we have enjoyed these made into pizza pockets using pepperoni slices, tomato sauce, and dairy-free mozzarella cheese (I used the same ratio as the filling for Plantain Pizza Pockets, page 73). Those ingredients won't "roll" into a stick, so they'll be more of a pocket or square. Bake and store the same as above. You can also do the same with other fillings such as sausage, egg, and cheese.

DIY Trail Mix

WHOLE 30   

SERVES:	PREP TIME:	COOK TIME:
3 to 6*	15 minutes	0 minutes

*MAKES: 1½ to 3 cups

This trail mix is easy to personalize and travels well in a lunch box or on a trip. My boys love making this their own, so I set out the options and let them mix and match. To make sure the end result is not just all sweet ingredients and has the staying power of healthy fats, I use the ratios given at right. If you need a nut-free option, lean into the seed and coconut healthy fats.

▸ **Note: If you are on a Whole30, this is a great emergency or travel food. To make this Whole30-compatible, mix and match as desired from the fruit and healthy fats category, making sure not to use peanuts or any fruit with added sugar. Leave out the cacao nibs and chocolate chips.**

1 to 1½ cups healthy fats: peanuts, cashews, almonds, walnuts, pecans, roasted sunflower seeds, pumpkin seeds, large coconut flakes

½ to 1 cup dried or freeze-dried fruit: Raisins, cranberries, pineapple, mango, apples, freeze-dried strawberries, mango, raspberries, bananas

Optional: ½ cup sweet treat: cacao nibs, dairy-free chocolate chips, or white chocolate chips

In a medium bowl, combine your selections from each category. Store the mix in a tightly sealed container at room temperature for up to 2 months.

OUR FAVORITE MIXES

Tropical Twist

½ cup almonds + ½ cup cashews + ½ cup coconut flakes + ½ cup dried pineapple + ½ cup dried mango. Optional: Add ¼ to ½ cup white chocolate chips.

Berry Nice

½ cup almonds + ½ cup pecans + 1 cup total freeze-dried strawberries/blueberries/raspberries (we use a mixture or you could use just one) + ½ cup chocolate chips or white chocolate chips.

Classic Mix

½ cup walnuts + ½ cup almonds + ¼ cup pumpkin seeds + ¼ cup sunflower seeds + ½ cup raisins + ½ cup chocolate chips.

Chunky Monkey

½ cup walnuts + ½ cup peanuts + ½ cup coconut flakes + 1 cup banana chips + ½ cup raisins + ½ cup chocolate chips.

Paleo Club Crackers

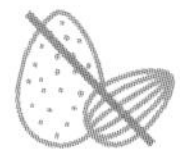   

MAKES ABOUT:	PREP TIME:	COOK TIME:
30 crackers	15 minutes	10 minutes

Note: We prefer this version with the almond flour, as it creates an amazing melt-in-your-mouth texture, but I also share a nut-free variation that has more of a thin, crispy texture.

My kids subsisted on crackers for at least a year or two of their lives. My pickiest son would walk around grazing on a bowl full of them most days, yet he was still always hungry. But these crackers are nutrient-dense with healthy fats and grain-free flours, and if I could show you the look on my boys' faces when they tried them for the first time—they were thrilled! So very easy and perfect for any lunch box or after-school snack.

¾ cup tapioca flour
½ cup almond flour (see Variation)
2 tablespoons coconut flour
1½ teaspoons baking powder
1½ teaspoons coconut sugar
½ teaspoon salt
½ cup Ghee (page 266), or store-bought, soft but not melted
1 tablespoon extra-light-tasting olive oil

1 Preheat the oven to 400°F.

2 In a food processor, combine the flours, baking powder, sugar, and ¼ teaspoon of the salt and pulse until combined. Add 3 tablespoons of the ghee and the olive oil. Pulse again until combined.

3 With the food processor running, add 4½ tablespoons of water, 1 tablespoon at a time. The dough is ready when it comes together into a ball. Add extra water if needed, but for me it always lands at 4½ tablespoons.

4 Lay out a large piece of parchment paper and place the dough on top. Top the dough with another piece of parchment paper.

recipe continues

Use a rolling pin to roll out the dough between the two pieces of parchment until the dough is about 1/4 inch thick. Don't roll any thinner, or the crackers will be crumbly. Use a knife or pizza cutter to cut the dough into 1 x 2-inch rectangles. Poke each rectangle 2 or 3 times with a fork for more even baking.

5 Bake for 9 to 11 minutes, until the edges are golden. Let the crackers cool on the counter.

6 Meanwhile, melt the remaining 5 tablespoons ghee and brush it over the tops of the cooked crackers. Sprinkle with the remaining 1/4 teaspoon salt.

7 Store the cooled crackers in a sealed container in the pantry for up to 1 week.

Can be frozen in a sealed container for up to 3 months to extend shelf life.

NUT-FREE VARIATION

Use 3/4 cup tapioca flour + 1/4 cup cassava flour instead of the almond + tapioca flour. Increase the amount of ghee in the batter to 4 tablespoons and the water to 5 tablespoons. Follow the rest of the instructions as written.

Homemade Microwave Popcorn

SERVES:	PREP TIME:	COOK TIME:
8*	5 minutes	2½ to 3 minutes

*MAKES: 8 cups

I adored popcorn as a child so much that I asked for (and received) a large box of movie theater-style microwave popcorn for all of my birthdays from ages seven to twelve. My mom sewed a decal of popcorn on my section of a family wall-hanging quilt—that's how much I loved popcorn. I was skeptical that homemade popcorn without a lot of terrible ingredients could be worth my time. But this version has the taste you love in the microwave stuff minus the bad stuff, and all of us have loved it right from the start. Not only is it delicious, but it's much more affordable than healthy prepackaged brands. The popcorn and nut salt is optional, but it really makes this taste like commercial popcorn, so I would recommend it. I have found it on Amazon.

1 lunch-sized brown paper bag
⅓ cup popcorn kernels
3 tablespoons Ghee (page 266) or coconut oil, or a blend of each (I prefer a 50-50 mix)
Optional: Popcorn and nut salt, for serving

1 Into the paper bag, pour the popcorn kernels and top them with the ghee and/or coconut oil. Fold the top of the bag over about 1 inch and repeat once more to create a seal.

2 Place the bag on a plate in the microwave. This will help prevent oil from seeping out on your turntable. Microwave the bag for 2½ to 3 minutes, or until the popping begins to slow to a pop every couple seconds. It's better to pull out the bag earlier than to leave it in too long and end up with a bag of burnt popcorn. Be careful when removing the plate from the microwave; it will be hot!

3 Season to taste with popcorn and nut salt or regular salt.

Paleo Vanilla Wafers

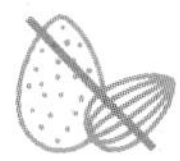

SERVES:	PREP TIME:	COOK TIME:
40*	20 minutes	10 minutes

*MAKES: 40 cookies

▸ Note: These cookies are delicious with ¼ to ⅓ cup mini chocolate chips added to the dough. You can also enjoy the dough by itself as an edible cookie dough—no baking needed! And while we prefer the rich flavor of the almond flour, you can use ¾ cup cassava flour + ½ cup tapioca flour instead of the almond flour + tapioca flour, using only 2 tablespoons of olive oil. Roll the nut-free dough into balls for best-looking results (otherwise, these nut-free cookies will be slightly bumpy in texture once baked). Freeze for 10 minutes before baking.

My whole family did the happy dance when I created this healthier, homemade version of the classic childhood cookie. My kids swore they tasted like the real deal, and I was dancing because they are budget-friendly, sweetened with only honey, have a decent dose of healthy fats, and are way more satiating than the average cookie. They're also a cinch to make, call for minimal ingredients, and are portable, making them great for lunch boxes or road trips.

1 cup almond flour (see Note)
1 cup tapioca flour
1 tablespoon baking powder
½ teaspoon salt
⅓ cup honey
¼ cup Ghee (page 266), or store-bought, soft but not melted
3 tablespoons extra-light-tasting olive oil or coconut oil
1 tablespoon vanilla extract

1 Preheat the oven to 325°F. Line a baking sheet with parchment paper and set aside. In a food processor, combine the flours, baking powder, and salt and process until mixed. Add the honey, ghee, oil, and vanilla and process until the dough comes together, about 30 seconds.

2 Scoop the dough onto the prepared baking sheet in ½-tablespoon scoops—don't make these too big. Use a ½-tablespoon cookie scoop, or put all the dough in a disposable sandwich bag. Twist the top of the bag tight, pushing the dough down into the opposite bag corner like a frosting piping bag. Cut off the tip of the corner that is not twisted shut, and then squeeze the dough onto the parchment paper in nickel-size amounts. Space the scoops of dough at least 1 inch apart, using two baking sheets if needed.

Freeze in a sealed container for up to 3 months.

3 Bake for 13 to 15 minutes, until the cookies are crispy with light-brown edges. Let the cookies cool on the baking sheet, then store them in a sealed container in the pantry for up to 2 weeks.

Chocolate Paleo Pudding & Fruit Dip

SERVES:	PREP TIME:	CHILL TIME:
8*	5 to 10 minutes	2 hours

*MAKES: 8 (½-cup) servings

This pudding and fruit dip has 2 CUPS of cauliflower in it, is only sweetened by honey, and my boys can't get enough of it. I do internal cartwheels every time they request it, which is almost weekly. It makes a great snack or lunch box side as it's veggie-based and filled with healthy fats that make it satiating and decrease cravings. I love using steam-in-a-bag riced cauliflower to simplify the preparation. Once the cauliflower is steamed, all you have to do is blend and chill.

1 (15-ounce) can coconut cream, chilled for at least 24 hours
2 cups steamed riced cauliflower
¼ cup cocoa powder
¼ cup nut or sun butter
¼ cup honey
1 teaspoon vanilla extract

1 Drain off any liquid from the coconut cream and set aside to use in smoothies or another recipe. In a blender, combine the solid part of the coconut cream, the cauliflower, cocoa powder, nut butter, honey, and vanilla and blend until the mixture is smooth and creamy, about 1 to 2 minutes. If you have a high-powered mixer like a Vitamix, use no higher than a medium speed for this; high speeds will make it chunky.

2 You can enjoy this immediately, but we prefer it chilled in the fridge for 2 hours to thicken its consistency. I like to pour the pudding into 8 individual ramekins or plastic reusable cups so it's easy to grab from the fridge. It can be stored for up to 2 weeks.

Fruit Juice Gelatin

WHOLE 30  	SERVES: 6 to 8*	PREP TIME: 10 minutes	CHILL TIME: 3 hours

*MAKES: 6 (½-cup) servings or 8 (⅓-cup) servings

I grew up in the eighties and nineties when Jell-O cups were a THING. I have several boys who love Jell-O and were begging for this recipe. I was shocked by how easy they are to re-create! And so much fun! I love them unsweetened, but you can sweeten a bit, if desired. Play around with your juice choices. We love more flavorful juices like white peach-grape juice or all-juice fruit punch, with a touch (like 1 cup) of a tart juice like tart cherry.

4 cups juice of choice
2 (0.25-ounce) packets or 1½ tablespoons gelatin
2 to 3 tablespoons granulated sweetener, if desired

1 In a medium saucepan, bring 3 cups of juice to a boil over high heat. Into a medium bowl, pour the remaining 1 cup juice and sprinkle the gelatin over the top. The gelatin will "bloom," absorbing the juice and growing slightly in size.

2 Whisk the boiling juice into the gelatin mixture. Add the sweetener (if using) and whisk again. Whisk for 5 minutes. Don't cut corners on this—the 5 minutes are important to fully dissolve the gelatin.

3 After 5 minutes, pour the mixture evenly into 6 to 8 containers of your choice (about ½ cup in each for 6 servings or ⅓ cup in each for 8 servings). I use glass or plastic ½-cup containers that are easy to pack in lunches. Chill the gelatin in the fridge for 3 hours before serving. These can be stored in the fridge for up to 3 weeks.

Baked Apple Chips

WHOLE 30  

SERVES:	PREP TIME:	COOK TIME:
4	10 minutes	3 hours

These crisp apple chips are made with simple ingredients but have a satisfying flavor. They make a fun travel or lunch box snack. Store-bought apple chips can be pricey and are not Whole30-compatible, but these homemade ones are both affordable and allowed on Whole30. I highly recommend using a mandoline slicer to get them nice and thin. I set mine to 2-millimeter thickness. You can use whatever apples you have on hand and need to use up. We enjoy eating these as is, but you can also top with a sprinkle of cinnamon.

2 large apples of choice
2 tablespoons fresh lemon juice
1 tablespoon ground cinnamon (optional)

1 Preheat the oven to 200°F. Line two baking sheets with parchment and set aside.

2 Using a mandoline or sharp knife, slice the apples very thin, about 2 millimeters. I do not peel or core them before I do this. In a small bowl, toss the apples with the lemon juice to prevent them from browning, and with the cinnamon, if desired. Arrange the apple slices in a single layer on the prepared baking sheet.

3 Bake for 1½ hours, flip, and then bake 1½ hours more. You can place both baking pans in the same oven, just make sure to switch the lower one to the higher shelf and vice versa halfway through the baking time so that they cook evenly. Turn off the oven and *leave the apples to cool in the oven*. This will help them get a little crunchier as they cool. The apple chips will not be crispy immediately after cooking but will crisp once they cool to room temperature.

4 The tricky part with apple chips is keeping them crunchy, as they can easily go soft after about a day if exposed to air. Store them in a zip-top bag, pushing out as much air as possible and sealing the bag almost all the way. Then insert a straw in the small gap of the zip top that's not sealed and suck out any air. Suck in until you can't anymore, and then quickly remove the straw and finish sealing the bag. Each time you open the bag, remove the air again to keep them crispy. Stored this way, the chips will last for up to 2 weeks at room temperature.

Roasted Snack Mix

WHOLE 30  	SERVES: 4*	PREP TIME: 10 minutes	COOK TIME: 1 hour

*MAKES: 4 cups

Roasted nuts are already delicious, but add in some different flavor profiles, and they're elevated to the next level. Packaged Paleo seasoned snack mixes are very pricey, but it's so easy to make them on your own. This recipe is infinitely flexible. You can alter the mix of nuts, add things like seeds or Plantain Chips (page 164), or even non-Whole30 ingredients such as gluten-free pretzels or Chex cereal. Make it yours!

Note: The plantain chips, pretzels, and cereal will absorb the flavor more than the dense nuts. If you are doing a mix with just nuts and seeds, I recommend increasing the seasoning recipe 1½ times to keep things flavorful.

4 cups mixed nuts, seeds, Plantain Chips (page 164) or store-bought, gluten-free pretzels, or Chex cereal
3 tablespoons melted Ghee (page 266), or store-bought
Seasonings (recipes below)

SEASONINGS

Ranch Mix: 2 tablespoons Ranch Seasoning (page 265)
Bold Mix: 2 tablespoons coconut aminos, 1 teaspoon seasoned salt, 1 teaspoon garlic powder, and 1 teaspoon onion powder
Cinnamon-Sugar Mix: 1 tablespoon vanilla extract, 2 tablespoons coconut or maple sugar, 1 teaspoon ground cinnamon, ¼ teaspoon salt
Everything Bagel Mix: 1 egg white, whisked until frothy, in place of ghee, plus 2 tablespoons everything bagel seasoning.

1. Preheat the oven to 250°F. Line a baking sheet with parchment paper and set aside. In a medium bowl, combine the nut mixture and melted ghee or egg white. Stir in your seasonings of choice. If the seasoning you've chosen has any liquid in it (coconut aminos or vanilla), mix that with the nuts first. Then, once combined, add the dry seasonings and mix well.

2. Spread the mixture evenly over the prepared baking sheet and bake for 1 hour, until fragrant and lightly browned.

3. Store in a sealed container in the pantry for up to 1 month.

Soups and Green Salads

Budget Beef Stew

WHOLE 30   	SERVES: 8*	PREP TIME: 25 minutes	COOK TIME: 40 minutes

*Servings are 1½ cups each

Beef stew was one of my comfort food favorites as a kid. But stew meat can be pricey, so I created this affordable version of beef stew with ground beef. It tastes just as delicious and has the fantastic bonus of having hidden veggies in the broth! My boys aren't fans of cauliflower, but they haven't been able to sniff it out yet. I love the simplicity of making this in the Instant Pot, but it also works great on the stove or in a slow cooker. Such a fantastic, nourishing, hearty stew! We love this with my Paleo Dinner Rolls (page 236) and a side salad.

2 pounds ground beef
4 cups beef broth or bone broth
1 (15-ounce) can tomato sauce
2 tablespoons dried minced onion
1 tablespoon salt
2 teaspoons garlic powder
1 teaspoon dried thyme
½ teaspoon ground black pepper
1 dried bay leaf
1 pound Yukon gold or russet potatoes, chopped
3 medium or 2 large fresh carrots, chopped
1 large head fresh cauliflower, leaves removed and head chopped into large florets

1 In a large pot over medium heat on the stove or in an Instant Pot on Sauté, cook the ground beef until it is browned and no longer pink, about 10 minutes.

2 In a large bowl, stir together the broth, tomato sauce, dried onion, salt, garlic powder, thyme, pepper, and bay leaf.

recipe continues

3 When the meat is browned, combine all of the ingredients in the pot, the Instant Pot, or a slow cooker.

4 **TO COOK ON THE STOVE:** Bring the mixture to a boil, reduce to a simmer over medium heat, and cook, covered, for 30 minutes, until the veggies are tender.

5 **TO COOK IN AN INSTANT POT:** Seal the Instant Pot lid and cook on the Stew setting for 25 minutes. Manually release the steam.

6 **TO COOK IN A SLOW COOKER:** Fasten the lid and cook on low for 8 hours or on high for 4 hours.

7 **FOR ALL COOKING METHODS:** Once the cooking time is finished, remove the bay leaf. Scoop out all the cauliflower florets and some of the broth and puree them in a blender or food processor at a high speed until creamy. Return the mixture to the stew and stir until well combined.

Store in a sealed container and freeze for up to 3 months. We prefer to do this in individual portions.

Chicken Fajita Soup

WHOLE 30					SERVES: 6	PREP TIME: 10 minutes	COOK TIME: 20 minutes

Make It a Meal

We enjoy this with a side of my Cilantro Salsa Slaw (page 243) and fruit.

I love this hearty soup that comes together easily from mostly frozen and canned veggies. I'm a spice wimp, so the recipe is written with only a mild kick to it. You are welcome to amp up the spice like my second son, who promptly stirs in 2 extra tablespoons of jalapeños. If you aren't on a Whole30, this is also delicious with a can of black beans, rinsed, or 1 to 2 cups of frozen corn (add an equal amount of additional broth if using these add-ins). We love it served with avocado, chopped fresh cilantro, and Tostones (page 224) or Plantain Chips (page 164).

- 2 tablespoons Ghee (page 266), or store-bought
- 1 medium yellow onion, diced
- 1½ pounds boneless, skinless chicken breasts, trimmed
- 4½ to 5½ cups chicken broth or bone broth (4½ cups for Instant Pot, 5½ cups for stovetop)
- 2 (15-ounce) cans diced tomatoes with green chiles
- 1 pound frozen or fresh bell peppers, sliced
- 2 cups frozen or fresh riced cauliflower
- 1 to 4 tablespoons chopped canned or fresh jalapeños, depending on your heat preference
- 1 tablespoon chili powder
- 1 teaspoon salt
- 1 teaspoon ground cumin
- ½ teaspoon paprika
- **Optional:** chopped fresh cilantro, sliced fresh avocado, and Tostones (page 224) or Plantain Chips (page 164), for topping

1 In a large pot over medium heat or in an Instant Pot on Sauté, melt the ghee. Add the onion and cook until translucent, about 5 minutes. Add the chicken, broth, tomatoes, bell peppers, cauliflower, jalapeños, chili powder, salt, cumin, and paprika. Bring

recipe continues

Chicken Fajita Soup,
continued

the mixture to a boil, cover, and cook for 20 minutes, until the chicken is cooked through and the veggies are tender. If using an Instant Pot, cook on Soup for 20 minutes.

2 Transfer the chicken from the pot and shred. I prefer to use a hand or standing mixer to shred. Cover the bowl with a towel to minimize mess and mix for 1 to 2 minutes until it's just shredded. Or transfer the chicken to a cutting board and use two forks to shred the meat. Return the meat to the pot and serve the soup with your toppings of choice.

Store in individual servings in sealed containers. Freeze for up to 3 months.

Creamy Tomato Soup

WHOLE 30					SERVES: 6*	PREP TIME: 5 minutes	COOK TIME: 20 minutes

*Servings are 1 cup each

For most of my life, I didn't like tomato soup. I thought it was possibly the most boring soup out there. Then, ironically, I married a man who loved it. I finally understood why when I went to a soup and sandwich shop during a Ragnar relay race, and I fell in love with their Creamy Basil Tomato Soup. I was so happy to create this Whole30 version! The ingredients are simple, and this recipe works beautifully with canned goods and frozen veggies for a meal that comes together in less than 30 minutes. The carrots are optional but will help the canned tomatoes in the soup taste less acidic.

¼ cup plus 2 tablespoons Ghee (page 266)
1 medium yellow onion, chopped
4 fresh garlic cloves, chopped
2 (15-ounce) cans diced tomatoes
3 cups fresh or frozen riced cauliflower
2 large fresh carrots, thinly sliced (optional)
1 (6-ounce) can tomato paste
½ cup chicken broth or bone broth
1 teaspoon salt
1 cup packed fresh basil, or 1 tablespoon dried basil
1½ cups full-fat coconut milk

1 In a large pot, melt the ghee over medium heat. Add the onion and garlic and cook until the onion is translucent, 4 to 5 minutes.

2 Add the tomatoes, cauliflower, carrots (If using), tomato paste, broth, and salt. If using fresh basil, stir it in now. If using dried, hold off. Increase the heat to high and cook for 10 minutes, until the tomatoes and cauliflower are tender. Stir regularly to prevent burning.

3 Carefully transfer the soup to a blender and add the coconut milk and dried basil, if using. Blend until smooth.

Store in a sealed container and freeze for up to 3 months. We prefer to do this in individual portions.

Creamy Chicken Chowder

WHOLE 30   	SERVES: 6*	PREP TIME: 15 minutes	COOK TIME: 20 to 30 minutes**

*Servings are 1½ cups each
**COOK TIME: 20 minutes in Instant Pot; 30 minutes for stovetop method

Make It a Meal

We love eating this with a Caesar Salad (page 204, sans chicken), Paleo Dinner Rolls (page 236, if not on Whole30), and fruit.

I love a good, creamy soup because it's so comforting. This one has an extra veggie boost thanks to the cauliflower, which gives it a nice, creamy texture without an overwhelming taste of cauliflower. My boys have never even noticed!

3 tablespoons Ghee (page 266), or store-bought
1 medium yellow or white onion, diced
1 tablespoon minced fresh garlic
2½ to 3½ cups chicken broth or bone broth (2½ cups for Instant Pot, 3½ cups for stovetop)
2 tablespoons Flavor Boost Powder (page 258)
1 teaspoon garlic salt
1 pound boneless, skinless chicken breasts, excess fat trimmed
3 fresh celery hearts, chopped
2 cups fresh baby carrots or 3 large carrots, chopped
1 pound white or yellow potatoes (about 4 medium potatoes), chopped
2 cups riced cauliflower
½ cup full-fat coconut milk or other dairy-free milk
1½ cups frozen peas

1 In an Instant Pot on Sauté or in a large pot over medium heat, melt the ghee. Add the onion and garlic and cook until the onion is translucent, about 5 minutes. In a medium bowl, combine the broth, flavor boost powder, and garlic salt. Once the onion is translucent, add the chicken breasts, followed by the celery, carrots, and potatoes. Pour the broth mixture into the pot.

recipe continues

2 If using an Instant Pot, seal and cook on Soup for 20 minutes. If cooking on the stove, bring the soup to a boil then reduce to a simmer and partially cover. Simmer for 30 minutes, or until the chicken is no longer pink inside.

3 Steam the cauliflower. I like to buy steam-in-a-bag frozen veggies for this so I can just throw it in the microwave. Otherwise, you can add the cauliflower to a glass dish, add 2 tablespoons water, cover with microwave-safe plastic wrap, and steam in the microwave for 4 minutes.

4 Once the chicken is cooked through, combine the steamed cauliflower, milk, and 1 cup of broth from the soup pot in a food processor or blender. Blend until very smooth.

5 Remove the chicken from the pot and shred. I like to do this in a large bowl with a hand mixer or in the bowl of my standing mixer. Cover the bowl with a towel to minimize mess and mix for 1 to 2 minutes until just shredded. You can also put the chicken on a cutting board and use two forks to pull the meat in opposite directions.

6 Add the chicken, cauliflower mixture, and frozen peas to the hot soup. Stir until combined and enjoy.

Freeze in a sealed container for up to 3 months.

Lasagna Soup

WHOLE 30    

SERVES:	PREP TIME:	COOK TIME:
6	10 minutes	20 minutes

Pictured on page 202.

▸ **Note: For a Whole30 variation, use 24 ounces drained hearts of palm instead of the pasta. For the cheese, nut-based cheese is allowed on Whole30 if the ingredients are compatible.**

Want the flavor and heartiness of lasagna in only 30 minutes and in a one-pot meal? This soup has your name on it. I turn to this favorite when we don't have much time to get dinner on the table, and it is easy enough for my teens to make. This is the comfort of lasagna wrapped up in a warm, cozy soup.

1 (28-ounce) can diced tomatoes
2 cups steamed riced cauliflower
1¼ cups full-fat coconut milk
1 (6-ounce) can tomato paste
2 teaspoons garlic salt
1½ teaspoons dried basil
1 tablespoon olive oil
1 small yellow onion, chopped
1 tablespoon minced fresh garlic
1 pound ground meat of choice or ground Italian sausage
1 tablespoon Italian seasoning (omit if using seasoned sausage)
2 to 4 cups chicken or beef broth or bone broth
8 ounces gluten-free pasta of choice (omit for Whole30)
Optional: 1 to 2 cups shredded dairy-free mozzarella cheese, for serving

1 In a blender or food processor, combine the tomatoes, cauliflower, coconut milk, tomato paste, garlic salt, and basil and blend until the mixture is very smooth. Set aside.

2 In a large soup pot, heat the oil over medium heat. Add the onion, garlic, and ground meat seasoned with the Italian seasoning, unless you're using seasoned sausage. Cook until the onion is translucent and the meat is no longer pink in the center, about 10 minutes.

3 Add the tomato mixture, 2 cups broth, and pasta to the soup pot and increase the heat to high. Cook, covered, for 8 to 10 minutes, stirring occasionally, until the pasta is tender. If the soup is too thick, add up to 2 more cups of broth. Top with the cheese, if desired, and serve.

Freeze in a sealed container for up to 3 months.

Blackened Chicken Caesar Salad with Creamy Whole30 Dressing

WHOLE 30 	SERVES: 4	PREP TIME: 20 minutes	COOK TIME: 20 minutes

Pictured on page 203

Note: To make this nut-free, simply omit the cashews.

Creamy Caesar dressing was the first salad dressing my boys came to love, which became a bridge to enjoying salad in general. But it was an expensive Whole30-compatible dressing that was hard to find. I was determined to create my own version that was affordable and made with easy-to-find ingredients. This dressing mimics a creamy Caesar dressing brand we love and does not have anchovies in it like traditional Caesar dressing. The blackened chicken is fast and simple to make, and it's delicious as a main dish, too. This is a filling, family-sized salad we all enjoy, and it has even been packed in lunch boxes by request.

FOR THE BLACKENED CHICKEN:

- 1 teaspoon paprika
- ½ teaspoon dried thyme
- ¼ teaspoon salt
- ½ teaspoon ground black pepper
- ¼ teaspoon onion powder
- ½ teaspoon ground cumin
- 1 pound boneless, skinless chicken breasts, trimmed of excess fat
- 1 tablespoon extra-virgin olive or avocado oil

FOR THE CREAMY CAESAR DRESSING:

- 1 cup extra-light-tasting olive oil
- 1 large egg
- 3 tablespoons lemon juice
- 1 tablespoon yellow mustard
- 1½ teaspoons white vinegar
- 1½ teaspoons coconut aminos
- 1½ teaspoons ground black pepper
- ½ teaspoon onion powder
- ½ teaspoon garlic powder
- ¼ teaspoon salt

FOR THE SALAD:

1 large head fresh romaine lettuce, cut into pieces and washed
2 large fresh avocados, sliced
½ cup chopped salted cashews (see Note)
½ cup roasted and salted sunflower seeds

1 **MAKE THE CHICKEN:** You can do this on the grill or on the stove. If using a grill, preheat it to 450°F.

2 In a small bowl, combine the paprika, thyme, salt, pepper, onion powder, and cumin. Cut the chicken in half horizontally. Rub the chicken with the blackening spice mix, taking care to coat it as evenly as possible on all sides.

3 Grill for 5 to 6 minutes on each side until the meat reaches an internal temperature of 165°F.

4 Alternatively, in a large skillet, heat the oil over medium-high heat. When the oil is hot, add the chicken and don't move it for 4 to 5 minutes. The heat will create the "blackened" effect on the chicken, giving it its flavorful crust. Flip the chicken over and cook for 5 minutes more, until the chicken has a nice crust and is no longer pink in the center. Set aside to cool.

5 **MAKE THE DRESSING:** In a wide-mouth jar or other tall, narrow container that is just larger than the head of your immersion blender, combine the olive oil, egg, lemon juice, mustard, vinegar, coconut aminos, pepper, onion powder, garlic powder, and salt. Let the contents sit for a few minutes so the egg sinks to the bottom. Put the immersion head into the container directly on top of the egg yolk. Wait 10 seconds then turn the blender on high, still holding it down over the yolk. Blend for 10 seconds and then slowly pull up through the rest of the mixture to emulsify. To ensure emulsification, don't rush these steps!

6 **MAKE THE SALAD:** After the chicken has rested for at least 10 minutes, cut it into strips. Divide the chicken, lettuce, avocado, cashews, and sunflower seeds into 4 bowls. Drizzle each with ¼ to ⅓ cup of dressing. Extra dressing can be stored in the fridge for up to 2 weeks. If any portion of the salad will be saved for later, do not dress it until you're ready to eat it.

Cobb Salad

WHOLE 30   	SERVES:	PREP TIME:	COOK TIME:
	1	15 minutes	0 minutes

▼ **Note: Want to prep these ahead of time? Combine all the ingredients except the diced tomato and dressing in a sealed container. Wait to toss them with the salad when you're ready to eat. To make this salad nut-free and egg-free, simply omit the chopped cashews and hard-boiled egg.**

This is my go-to salad, and I eat it almost weekly. I love using leftover chicken like Our Favorite Chicken Strips (page 70) or Blackened Chicken (page 204). I used to miss the crunch of croutons in my Whole30 salads, but adding seeds and/or nuts is the perfect solution. And my Whole30 Date Mustard Sauce (page 250) is just delicious on a salad. Feel free to make this salad your own by changing up the add-ins as your heart desires.

2 packed cups chopped fresh romaine lettuce
1 cup chopped cooked chicken
½ fresh avocado, peeled and chopped
1 hard-boiled egg, sliced (see Note)
1 or 2 slices cooked bacon, crumbled
¼ cup diced fresh tomato
2 tablespoons chopped salted cashews (see Note)
2 tablespoons pumpkin or sunflower seeds
2 tablespoons diced sweet onion
½ teaspoon garlic salt
½ cup Whole30 Date Mustard Sauce (page 250)

In a medium bowl, toss together all the ingredients and drizzle with the dressing. Enjoy!

Fuji Chicken Apple Salad

WHOLE 30  

SERVES:	PREP TIME:	COOK TIME:
2	15 minutes	30 minutes

Similar to one at a well-known soup and salad restaurant, this light and sweet salad is big on veggies and flavor. You can use all arugula or all spring mix for the greens; I just like using a variety. If you use leftover grilled or steamed chicken, this comes together in a snap. If you are on a Whole30, don't use store-bought apple chips and double-check that your dried cranberries don't have added sugar or just use raisins.

▸ Note: To make this salad nut-free, replace the ¾ cup whole pecans with ½ cup of another seed of choice, such as pumpkin or sunflower seeds.

½ pound boneless, skinless chicken breasts, trimmed and cut into 2 or 3 pieces
2 teaspoons extra-light-tasting olive or avocado oil
¼ teaspoon salt
¼ teaspoon ground black pepper
½ cup Creamy Apple Dressing (page 259)
¾ cup whole pecans (see Note)
4 cups fresh baby arugula
4 cups fresh spring mix
1½ cups Baked Apple Chips (page 184), or store-bought
⅓ cup finely chopped fresh tomato
3 tablespoons finely chopped red onion
3 tablespoons raisins or dried cranberries
Garlic salt, to taste

1 Preheat the oven to 350°F. Line a baking sheet with parchment paper.

2 Rub the chicken with 1 teaspoon of oil and sprinkle with salt and pepper. Place the chicken on the prepared baking sheet and bake for 30 minutes.

3 While the chicken bakes, prepare the creamy apple dressing, if you haven't already. In a medium saucepan, heat the remaining 1 teaspoon oil over medium-low heat. Add the pecans and cook for 5 minutes, until crispy. Watch carefully so they don't burn. Set aside to cool.

4 Once the chicken is done, let it cool before chopping it into small cubes. Divide all the remaining ingredients between two medium bowls or plates. Top with the dressing right before eating. Sprinkle with garlic salt, to taste.

Side Dishes

Onion Rings

WHOLE 30

SERVES:	PREP TIME:	COOK TIME:
4	10 minutes	20 minutes

This classic doesn't disappoint with all of the crispy, delicious flavor of the original and none of the gluten or grains. My kids said they didn't like onion rings, but then I made these and now I need to double the batch every time just to get any for myself! I highly recommend serving these with my Whole30 Date Mustard Sauce (page 250). And if you are lucky enough to have leftovers, these are delicious as a salad topping.

▸ **Note: The batter will stick best when eggs are in the mixture. But if needed, you can use ½ cup canned coconut milk instead. You can also sub ¾ cup cassava flour for the tapioca and coconut flour.**

1 large white or yellow onion
½ cup tapioca flour (see Note)
¼ cup coconut flour (see Note)
1 teaspoon garlic powder
1 teaspoon onion powder
1 teaspoon salt
3 large eggs (see Note)
Coconut or avocado oil, for cooking
Optional: Whole30 Date Mustard Sauce (page 250) or dipping sauce of choice, for serving

1 Trim off both ends of the onion and remove the outer peel. Holding it on its side, slice the onion vertically to create large rings. Set aside.

2 In a small bowl, combine the flours, garlic powder, onion powder, and salt. In a separate small bowl, beat the eggs.

3 In a medium saucepan, heat a shallow amount (about ¼ inch) of oil over medium heat. One at a time, dip both sides of the onion rings in the egg, letting any excess drip off, and then press both sides into the flour mixture. Repeat the process, dipping the onion ring again into the egg and flour to double-batter the onion ring. Then carefully lay the battered rings into the oil.

4 Cook the onion rings until they're golden, about 4 minutes on each side, taking care not to crowd the pan. Transfer the cooked onion rings to a paper towel–lined plate. Repeat with the remaining onion slices and serve hot with your dipping sauce of choice (if using).

Broccoli Salad

WHOLE 30  	SERVES: 8	PREP TIME: 30 minutes	COOK TIME: 0 minutes

▸ Note: To make this nut-free, simply omit the almonds and cashews.

This one is always a hit among Whole30ers and non-Whole30ers alike. It's more interesting than just raw veggies and more portable than hot ones. The amount of add-ins (fruit, nuts, seeds) can easily be adjusted to your preference. If you're out of raisins, you can substitute an equal amount of finely chopped apples. Can't find an affordable Whole30-compatible bacon? The salad is delicious without it. This is a great recipe for picnics, potlucks, or camping.

6 cups fresh broccoli florets (about 2 large heads broccoli)
2 cups store-bought broccoli slaw or another 2 cups broccoli florets
8 slices bacon, cooked and crumbled (optional)
1 cup red seedless grapes, halved
½ cup sliced almonds or chopped cashews (see Note)
½ cup sunflower seeds
½ cup raisins
1 cup Homemade Mayo (page 253)
¼ cup Date Paste (page 269)
2 tablespoons red wine vinegar

1 Trim the broccoli florets. I prefer mine small without a lot of stem, so I cut off larger florets and trim them into 1-inch bite-sized pieces, cutting in halves or in quarters with kitchen shears.

2 In a large bowl, combine the broccoli with the slaw, bacon (if using), grapes, nuts, seeds, and raisins. Set aside.

3 In a small bowl, combine the mayo, date paste, and red wine vinegar, whisking until smooth. Pour the dressing over the salad and toss to coat.

4 Serve cold and store leftovers in the fridge for up to 4 days. I like it even better the next day when the dressing has soaked into the veggies a bit.

Carrot Fries with Date Chipotle Sauce

WHOLE 30  	SERVES: 4	PREP TIME: 15 minutes	COOK TIME: 22 to 35 minutes*

*COOK TIME: 22 to 35 minutes, depending on cooking method

Note: If you are not on Whole30, you can also use 2 tablespoons pure maple syrup instead of the Date Paste for the sauce. To enjoy these carrot fries egg-free, use my Whole30 BBQ Sauce (page 256) in place of the Date Chipotle Sauce.

I used to get an appetizer just like this at one of my favorite restaurants, which has since shut down. Carrots can sometimes be a hard veggie to get excited about, and my hubby has flat out told me he's just not into them. But *these* are a wow! The sweet sauce with a kick is a clincher for the already awesome flavor of these carrot fries.

FOR THE CARROT FRIES:

1 pound whole fresh carrots
1 tablespoon extra-virgin olive oil
¼ cup tapioca or arrowroot flour
1 teaspoon garlic powder
1 teaspoon onion powder
½ teaspoon paprika
½ teaspoon salt

FOR THE DATE CHIPOTLE SAUCE (see Note):

½ cup Chipotle Mayo (page 253)
2 to 3 tablespoons Date Paste (page 269)

1 If baking in the oven instead of using an air fryer, preheat the oven to 400°F. Line a baking sheet with parchment paper and set aside.

2 Trim off the tops and tips of the carrots. Cut them into thin "fry" shapes. I leave the skins on. Steam for 5 minutes until tender. I do this in a stasher bag with 2 tablespoons water or a glass dish with 2 tablespoons of water covered with microwave-safe plastic

recipe continues

wrap in the microwave. Drain any excess water from the carrots and pat dry.

3 In a large bowl, toss the carrots in the olive oil. Sprinkle with the flour, garlic powder, onion powder, paprika, and salt and toss to coat.

Place the carrots in an air fryer basket and cook at 350°F for 15 minutes. Increase the heat to 400°F and cook 5 to 7 minutes more, until the fries are crispy. If the carrots are not in a single layer in your basket, gently toss them halfway through.

4 If baking, spread the carrots over the prepared baking sheet and bake for 20 minutes. Increase the heat to 425°F and bake 15 minutes more, until the fries are crispy.

5 **WHILE THE CARROTS ARE COOKING, MAKE THE DATE CHIPOTLE SAUCE:** In a medium bowl, combine the chipotle mayo with 2 tablespoons of date paste. Add more date paste, as desired, for added sweetness. Serve with the carrot fries.

Caulitots

WHOLE 30 		SERVES: 4	PREP TIME: 15 minutes	COOK TIME: 30 minutes

Pictured on pages 220–221

▸ **Note: I use steam-in-a-bag cauliflower to make this easy. Once the cauliflower is steamed, be sure to squeeze out *all* the excess water to get a nice, crispy texture. Potato starch will yield the crispiest results, but you can also substitute equal amounts of tapioca or arrowroot starch.**

I would like you to meet the tater tot's nutrient-dense and low-carb cousin, the Caulitot. I've found that changing the shape and texture of a veggie can help it be more appealing. These bite-sized tots are crispy and fun, and we love them paired with my Whole30 Date Mustard Sauce (page 250). They also freeze great, so go ahead and double-batch it.

2 cups steamed riced cauliflower (see Note)
1 large egg
¼ cup potato starch
2 tablespoons extra-virgin olive or avocado oil
1 teaspoon garlic salt
¼ teaspoon onion powder
Cooking oil spray
Salt, to taste

1 Preheat the oven to 375°F. Line a baking sheet with parchment paper.

2 Wrap the steamed cauliflower in a clean towel and squeeze out all the extra water. (I do this over the sink.) Just when you think you have it all out, squeeze some more! I'm usually able to squeeze out more than ½ cup water, with a little bit over a cup of the cauliflower left.

3 In a medium bowl, stir together the drained cauliflower with the egg, starch, oil, garlic salt, and onion powder. Spoon teaspoon-size dollops onto the prepared baking sheet. I make this easier with a 1-teaspoon baking scoop. Generously spray the tots with cooking oil spray.

4 Bake for 15 minutes, then flip. Generously spray the second side of the tots with cooking oil spray and increase the oven temperature to 400°F. Bake for 15 minutes more, until the tots are crispy on both sides. Salt to taste and serve.

Freeze the tots in a single layer until frozen, then store in a sealed container or reusable bag in the freezer for up to 3 months.

Cloud Drop Biscuits

SERVES:	PREP TIME:	COOK TIME:
14	10 minutes	10 minutes

▸ **Note: We prefer the three-flour mixture for the best results. For a nut-free modification, use 1 cup cassava flour instead of the three flours. They won't have the same cloud-like look to them, but they will still have a great texture.**

Sometimes you just need an easy dinner side, and these became an instant family favorite. No need to shape them; they come together quickly and have an incredible texture. They are also great topped with Sausage Gravy (page 121) or with Homemade Breakfast Sausage (page 57) as a breakfast sandwich.

¾ cup plus 2 tablespoons tapioca flour (see Note)
¾ cup almond flour (see Note)
⅓ cup coconut flour (see Note)
1 tablespoon baking powder
½ teaspoon salt
½ cup Ghee (page 266), soft but not melted
1 cup full-fat coconut milk

1. Preheat the oven to 450°F. Line a baking sheet with parchment paper and set aside.

2. In a medium bowl, stir together the flours, baking powder, and salt. Add the ghee and stir with a spoon or mix with your hands until the ghee is in pieces no larger than a pea. Add the coconut milk, stirring to combine. Let the mixture sit for 5 minutes to allow the coconut flour to thicken.

3. Drop the batter by the spoonful onto the prepared baking sheet. Bake for 10 minutes, or until light brown.

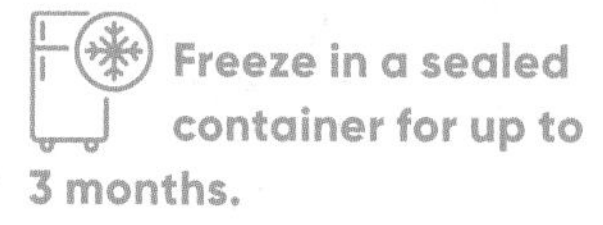

Tostones

WHOLE 30   	SERVES: 4	PREP TIME: 15 minutes	COOK TIME: 30 minutes

▸ Note: You could also coat the tostones with oil and pop them into an air fryer. But I don't really like the dry-fry result with this recipe. However, I do use the air fryer at 350°F for a few minutes to re-crisp the leftovers—and I always have leftovers since I usually double the batch and save half for later.

Tostones are one of my top-five favorite foods of all time. They are twice-cooked plantain slices common to Latin American and Caribbean cuisine. In South America, they are referred to as *patacones*, and some West African countries call them plantain crisps.

They call for just one ingredient, and my kids cheer when these flat, crispy circles of deliciousness come to the table. We love them with tacos, fajitas, or nachos. You can find plantains in the produce section, often by the bananas. You need to make sure to use green plantains for these, as the yellow ones will not get crispy and are more sweet than savory.

4 large green plantains
Avocado or coconut oil, for frying
Salt, to taste

1 Removing the peel of green plantains can be tricky. I recommend first trimming off the ends of the plantain, then cutting the plantain in half lengthwise. Score just through the peel on the side of each plantain half and use your thumb to start lifting the peel. Use that starting point to lift off all the peel.

2 Cut the peeled plantains into roughly 1-inch chunks. The bigger the pieces of plantain, the larger your tostones. I prefer 1-inch pieces because they cook quickly and yield a roughly 2-inch chip-size tostone.

3 In a large pan, heat about ¼ inch oil over medium heat. When the oil is hot, carefully place the plantain pieces flat-side down into the oil and cook until they are golden but not brown, 3 to

recipe continues

4 minutes. Using kitchen tongs or two forks, flip each piece, and continue cooking 3 to 4 minutes more, until golden on the second side.

4 Transfer the tostones to a piece of parchment paper. Cover with a second sheet of parchment and smash them flat. I do this with a kitchen mallet, but you can also use the bottom of a mug. They should easily smash into a nice, flat circle. If the plantains break apart when smashed, they weren't cooked long enough. Their thickness is up to you, but we like ours nice and thin. Do this all at once and right after removing the plantains from the pan. Once cooled, they will crumble when you smash them.

5 Place the smashed plantains back into the hot oil and cook for about 4 minutes, flipping halfway through, until they are hard and crispy. Transfer the tostones to a paper towel-lined plate, generously sprinkle with salt, and let them cool.

Freeze the tostones after smashing, and hold off on the second fry. I do so by laying them in a single layer and freezing until solid, then storing in a sealed container for up to 3 months. To cook, fry the tostones straight from frozen in ¼ inch oil over medium heat until crispy and hard, about 3 minutes per side. Blot on a paper towel, salt generously, and enjoy.

Breaded Potato Wedges

WHOLE 30  	SERVES: 4	PREP TIME: 10 minutes	COOK TIME: 15 to 35* minutes

*COOK TIME: 15 to 35 minutes, depending on cooking method

◎ Make It a Meal

These are a new family favorite and a great side that pairs well with Our Favorite Chicken Strips (page 70), Out-N-In Burger Bites (page 96), or Confetti Nuggets (page 86)

When I was pregnant, I used to frequent a particular fast-food restaurant known for their fried chicken. Their fries had this breading on them that made them taste amazing. Years later, I was determined to re-create those fries in a healthier way, and I'm happy to say that I've done it! Our family highly recommends cooking these in oil on the stove, but there are oven and air fryer versions as well.

1½ pounds russet potatoes
1 large egg
½ cup tapioca or arrowroot flour, or potato starch
1 tablespoon seasoned salt
½ teaspoon ground black pepper
½ tablespoon paprika
Optional: ½ cup high-heat oil of choice, such as coconut or avocado oil (if frying)
Optional: Cooking oil spray (if cooking in oven or air fryer)

1 **IF BAKING IN THE OVEN:** Preheat the oven to 400°F. Line a baking sheet with parchment paper and set aside.

2 Fill a medium bowl with cold water. Cut the potatoes into wedges or the fry shape of your choice. As you work, place the cut potatoes in the water to prevent them from oxidizing and turning brown. When you are done cutting the potatoes, drain the water and rinse the potatoes with additional cold water. Pat the potatoes dry.

3 In a medium bowl, beat the egg and add the potatoes. Stir until the potatoes are well coated. Transfer the potatoes to a colander to drain off any excess egg. Set aside.

recipe continues

Breaded Potato Wedges,
continued

4 In another medium bowl or in a large zip-top bag (my preference), combine the flour, salt, pepper, and paprika. Add the egg-coated potatoes to the flour mixture and combine well by stirring or sealing the bag and giving it a good shake.

Place breaded fries in air fryer basket. Spray generously with cooking oil spray. Air fry at 350°F for 7 minutes, flip or stir, and then air fry 8 minutes more, until crispy.

5 **TO COOK ON THE STOVETOP:** In a medium saucepan, heat the oil over medium-high heat. When the oil is hot, add the fries in a single layer to avoid crowding the pan. You will probably need to do this in a few batches. Cook for 5 minutes on each side until golden, then transfer the cooked fries to a paper towel–lined plate. Repeat with the remaining potatoes.

6 **TO COOK IN THE OVEN:** Lay the potatoes on the prepared baking sheet in a single layer. Spray generously with cooking oil spray. Cook for 20 minutes, flip, and then cook for 10 to 15 minutes more, until the potatoes are crispy on the outside and tender on the inside. The cook time will vary slightly depending on the size of your fries.

Freeze in a single layer on a cooling rack or baking sheet lined with parchment until frozen. Then store together in the freezer in a sealed container for up to 3 months.

Almond Green Bean Rice

WHOLE 30					SERVES: 4	PREP TIME: 5 minutes	COOK TIME: 25 minutes

▸ Note: Make this nut-free by simply omitting the almonds. You can also use roasted sunflower seeds in place of almonds to still add that crunch.

In our college days when money was tight and I didn't know how to cook, my husband and I lived on Rice-a-Roni and Hamburger Helper. I would make them "fancy" by adding green beans and roasted almonds. The first time he tried this recipe, my husband was immediately brought back to those days, which was 100 percent the goal. This easy side dish knocks down two veggies and is a great accompaniment to most meals.

3 tablespoons Ghee (page 266), or store-bought
2 cups fresh or frozen riced cauliflower
1½ tablespoons Flavor Boost Powder (page 258)
¾ cup chicken broth or bone broth
2 cups frozen or fresh green beans, trimmed
⅓ cup slivered almonds (see Note)

1 In a large saucepan, melt 2 tablespoons of ghee. Add the riced cauliflower and stir to combine. Sprinkle the cauliflower with the Flavor Boost Powder and stir again. Pour in the broth and green beans and bring to a boil. Boil for 15 minutes, or until the liquid in the pan is absorbed.

2 During the final 5 minutes of cooking time, in a small saucepan, melt the remaining 1 tablespoon ghee over medium-low heat. Add the sliced almonds and cook for 3 to 4 minutes, or until toasted.

3 Sprinkle the toasted almonds on top of the rice and serve.

Place in a sealed container and freeze for up to 3 months.

Balsamic Brussels Sprouts

WHOLE 30  

SERVES:	PREP TIME:	COOK TIME:
2	10 minutes	30 minutes

The first time I had Brussels sprouts, I was nineteen years old and they were boiled, slimy little green balls. I thought they were a veggie I could never love. But I have learned over the years that there is a way to enjoy almost every veggie with the right recipe and preparation. I now love Brussels sprouts. My trick is to steam them first so they are tender on the inside and then roast them until they're crispy. This balsamic sauce and bacon just put the whole thing over the top.

Air fry the seasoned Brussels sprouts at 350°F for 12 to 13 minutes, until crispy, stirring halfway through. Follow the remaining directions as written.

1 pound fresh Brussels sprouts, sliced in half
1 tablespoon extra-virgin olive oil
1 teaspoon seasoned salt
4 slices bacon (optional)
¼ cup balsamic vinegar
1 tablespoon Date Paste (page 269)

1. Preheat the oven to 425°F. Line a baking sheet with parchment paper and set aside.

2. In a zip-top bag, reusable silicone bag, or glass dish, combine the Brussels sprouts with 2 tablespoons water. If using a glass dish, cover it with microwavable plastic wrap. Microwave on high for 5 minutes.

3. Drain the excess water from the Brussels sprouts and transfer them to a medium bowl. Toss them with the oil and seasoned salt. Spread the Brussels sprouts over the prepared baking sheet and bake for 20 minutes, until crispy.

4. While the Brussels sprouts are roasting, in a large saucepan on the stove or an electric skillet, cook the bacon (if using) on medium heat. When crispy, flip, and cook until both sides are crispy.

5. In a small pot, simmer the balsamic vinegar over medium-low heat for 7 to 10 minutes, or until it has reduced to just 2 tablespoons. Stir in the date paste.

6. Drizzle the balsamic sauce over the Brussels sprouts and top with the crispy bacon.

Creamy Fruit Salad

WHOLE 30				SERVES: 8 to 10	PREP TIME: 10 minutes	COOK TIME: 0 minutes

I don't know if every child of the eighties or nineties grew up eating creamy fruit salad, but it was a central figure at every church potluck and special event in my young life. I was on a mission to make a creamy fruit salad that could be Whole30-compatible, and my boys fell in love with this one. I intentionally used canned, frozen, and fresh fruits that could be more easily found all year long so that this salad could be made in the winter as well. For the juice concentrate, we love something sweet like apple juice or apple-raspberry juice. The creamy part of the salad can be used as a fruit dip all on its own, too. It's sweet enough, but you can add ¼ cup honey if you want it sweeter (not Whole30-compatible). You can also use a pound of chopped fresh berries instead of the frozen mix.

1 (13-ounce) can chilled coconut cream, solid part only
¼ cup thawed frozen juice concentrate
1 tablespoon fresh lemon zest
1 (20-ounce) can pineapple tidbits or chunks, drained
1 (15-ounce) bag frozen mixed berries, thawed and drained
½ pound grapes, halved
1 large apple, cored and diced small

1 In the bowl of your mixer or using a handheld mixer over a medium bowl, beat together the coconut cream, juice concentrate, and lemon zest until smooth.

2 In a large bowl, combine the pineapple, berries, grapes, and apple. Gently fold the coconut cream mixture into the fruit. Don't overstir, or your fruit salad will be purple. Serve chilled.

Paleo All-Purpose Dough

SERVES:	PREP TIME:	COOK TIME:
12*	1 hour	15 to 30 minutes

*MAKES: 2 (14-inch) or 3 (9-inch) pizza crusts; 12 breadsticks; 12 crescent rolls; or 12 dinner rolls

▾ Note: I prefer the texture and flavor of the recipe with almond flour. But if you need a nut-free option, use ½ cup cassava flour + 1½ cups potato or tapioca flour instead of the almond flour + tapioca/potato flour. Brush the top of the dough with melted ghee before baking, as this dough tends to crack.

When I was growing up, my mom taught me how to make an easy French bread that we would gift to teachers, and it was eventually what won my husband's heart when we were dating. Making fresh bread is near and dear to my heart; however, Paleo bread-making is *tough* because gluten is not there to give the dough its structure.

I've worked harder on creating this delicious Paleo bread than on any other recipe in this book. I have recipe-tested it well over fifty times. But all the tinkering that went into making this fantastic dough has paid off, and it has so very many uses! This recipe yields a lot, because if you are going to go through the effort of making bread, you might as well get a lot of servings out of it. I've included recipes for how to turn the dough into breadsticks, pizza crust, crescent rolls, and dinner rolls, and it's the base for the Ham Rolls (page 167) and one of our favorite desserts, Churro Bites (page 310). Xanthan gum might be unfamiliar, but it's an important part of giving gluten-free dough its stretch. I find it in the bulk bins, natural food store, or online. No need for a lengthy rise time for this dough, as it doesn't have gluten to give it as big of a rise or structure. Even though it doesn't rise as high, it's still delicious!

1½ cups hot water
2 tablespoons instant yeast
1 tablespoon honey
1 cup potato flakes
1½ cups almond flour (see Note)
2 cups tapioca flour or potato starch (I prefer half and half)
2 tablespoons baking powder
1 teaspoon xanthan gum
1 teaspoon salt
½ cup melted Ghee (page 266), or extra-light-tasting olive oil
2 large eggs, beaten

1 Preheat the oven to 200°F.

2 In a medium bowl, combine ½ cup of hot water with the yeast and honey. Set aside while you prepare the rest of the dough, at least 5 minutes. The mixture should double or triple in size. This is called "proofing" your yeast, and seeing the yeast activity will help you feel more confident that your yeast will cause your dough to rise as it should.

3 In another medium bowl, stir together the potato flakes with the remaining 1 cup hot water. Set aside.

4 In a large bowl, combine the almond flour with 1½ cups of tapioca flour or potato starch, the baking powder, xanthan gum, and salt. Separately, stir together the ghee, eggs, potato flake mixture, and yeast mixture until combined. Add the ghee mixture to the dry ingredients and stir until well combined. The dough will be sticky.

Freeze cooled, cooked dough in a sealed container for up to 3 months.

5 Sprinkle the remaining ½ cup starch over your counter. Turn out the dough and knead until it's no longer sticky to the touch. Note: You are not kneading to help build structure as you would with gluten flours. Kneading gluten-free flours for structure is not needed; you're just bringing the dough together.

To Make Breadsticks:

1 Preheat the oven to 200°F.

2 Line a baking sheet with parchment paper. Divide the dough into 12 sections. Sprinkle the counter with tapioca or potato starch and roll the sections into long snakelike shapes, about 1 inch thick.

3 Place the shaped dough on the prepared pan and transfer to the oven. Immediately turn off the heat and let the dough proof for 30 minutes then remove it from the oven.

4 Preheat the oven to 400°F.

5 Bake the breadsticks for 15 minutes, until lightly browned. If desired, brush the baked breadsticks with melted ghee prior to serving.

recipe continues

Whole30 Potato Salad

WHOLE 30 		SERVES: 6 to 8	PREP TIME: 20 minutes	COOK TIME: 10 minutes

▾ Note: I don't love big chunks in my potato salad, so I cut the potatoes into small ½-inch cubes; I use my mini food processor to chop up the onion and pickles; and I grate the hard-boiled eggs with a cheese grater.

Potato salad is an American classic and such a great side dish to bring to any picnic or BBQ. It's easy to make and you can even make it ahead. Since it's good cold, it can also be a good lunch-on-the-go option (assuming you have a way to keep it chilled).

2 pounds russet potatoes, peeled and cubed
1 cup Homemade Mayo (page 253), or store-bought
1 tablespoon yellow mustard
1 teaspoon salt
¼ teaspoon ground black pepper
¼ cup finely chopped sweet onion
½ cup finely chopped dill pickles
2 fresh celery hearts, finely chopped
6 hard-boiled eggs, grated or chopped (see Note)
Paprika (optional)

1 Fill a large pot two-thirds full with water and bring to a boil over high heat. Add the potatoes and cook for 10 minutes, until fork tender. Drain the water and allow the potatoes to cool.

2 In a medium bowl, combine the mayo, mustard, salt, and pepper. Add the onion, pickles, and celery to the mayo mixture and stir to combine. Fold in the eggs.

3 In a large bowl, combine the mayo mixture and the potatoes, stirring gently until well combined. Sprinkle with paprika, if desired. Chill the salad for at least 2 to 3 hours before serving. Stays good in the fridge for up to 1 week.

Cilantro Salsa Slaw

WHOLE 30

SERVES:	PREP TIME:	COOK TIME:
6	10 minutes	0 minutes

▾ **Note: You can substitute 1 large tomato, finely chopped + 1 small jalapeño, seeded and finely chopped + 3 tablespoons finely chopped onion for the store-bought pico de gallo. Coleslaw doesn't keep well in the fridge, so do not add the dressing until ready to eat.**

Mexican food is possibly our family's favorite cuisine. I wanted to find a way to get more veggies on the table with a side dish that paired well with some of our favorite Mexican flavors. This slaw comes together quickly and is a fast add-on!

1 (14-ounce) bag classic coleslaw (shredded green cabbage and carrots)
1 cup pico de gallo
½ cup Cilantro Lime Ranch (page 252)
1 large fresh avocado
½ cup finely chopped fresh cilantro
½ small jalapeño, seeded and finely chopped (omit if making homemade pico de gallo per the Note, as that includes jalapeño)
½ teaspoon garlic salt
Optional: ½ cup corn or ½ cup rinsed canned black beans (not Whole30)

In a medium bowl, combine all of the ingredients, stirring until well combined. Eat immediately.

Cassava Flour Tortillas

SERVES:	PREP TIME:	COOK TIME:
6*	20 minutes	20 minutes

*MAKES: 12 taco (6-inch) or 6 burrito (10-inch) tortillas

For the first three years of eating Paleo, I couldn't find budget-friendly tortillas, so we went without them. Finally, I just decided to make my own—and my boys actually asked what they were supposed to do with them! Don't worry. We quickly figured it out and have since used them for lunch box sandwich wraps, breakfast burritos, tacos, and fajitas. Though there are now store-bought Paleo tortillas, the homemade ones are so much more affordable.

2 cups cassava flour
1 teaspoon salt
6 tablespoons extra-virgin olive oil
1 cup warm water

1 In a medium bowl, combine the flour and salt. Pour in the oil and mix well. Add the warm water and stir until well combined. The dough should be wet enough to hold together but not sticky.

2 Take a small ball of dough (3 tablespoons for a 6-inch taco-size tortilla or ⅓ cup for a 10-inch burrito-size tortilla) and place it between two sheets of parchment paper. Using a rolling pin, roll out the dough until it is very thin. Carefully remove the top piece of parchment paper. If the tortillas are cracking while being rolled out, return them to the dough, mix 1 or 2 tablespoons water into the dough, and try again.

3 In a medium pan, carefully transfer a tortilla to cook over medium heat. I do this by putting my hand under the remaining parchment paper, then quickly flipping the tortilla onto the pan.

4 Cook the tortilla for 1 minute before carefully peeling off the second piece of parchment. Flip and cook for 1 minute more on the other side, until the tortilla is firm but flexible. It will not brown. Pay close attention to the short cook time on these. If you overcook them, they will be hard and inflexible.

5 Store the tortillas by sandwiching each one between two pieces of parchment, then storing them inside a sealed zip-top bag. Doing so when they are warm will help them stay soft. Refrigerate leftovers, reheating them slightly to soften them before using.

Freeze with parchment between the tortillas in a sealed container for up to 3 months.

Crispy Freezer Veggies

WHOLE 30  

SERVES:	PREP TIME:	COOK TIME:
4	5 minutes	10 minutes

Note: Our favorite seasoning blend is Trader Joe's 21 Seasoning Salute. If your favorite seasoning blend has salt in it, omit the salt.

This is a dinner staple in our house. I keep veggies in my freezer at all times so they are ready to add to any meal that needs a veggie boost. Frozen veggies are budget-friendly, don't go out of season, and won't go bad in your crisper drawer. The secret is to steam them first before cooking them in oil; this makes them tender on the inside and crispy on the outside and is much faster than roasting.

1 (16-ounce) bag frozen veggies, such as broccoli, green beans, or mixed veggies like broccoli Normandy
2 tablespoons high-heat cooking oil such as coconut oil, avocado oil, or Ghee (page 266), or store-bought
½ teaspoon garlic salt
½ teaspoon seasoning blend of choice

1 To steam the veggies, I prefer to simplify this step by buying steam-in a-bag microwavable frozen veggies. But you can also do this by adding ¼ cup water and the veggies to a glass dish covered with microwave-safe plastic wrap or to a steamable reusable bag (like Stasher bags) and microwaving for 5 minutes. Drain off any excess water.

2 In a medium saucepan, heat the oil over medium-high heat. Once hot, add the veggies and sprinkle them with garlic salt and seasoning. Don't stir; let them get nice and crispy for about 6 to 7 minutes. Then flip and cook the other side for 5 to 6 minutes more.

Steam and season as above. Then air fry at 350°F for 12 to 13 minutes, until crispy.

TACO

Sauces and Seasonings

Whole30 Date Mustard Sauce

WHOLE 30  

MAKES:	PREP TIME:	COOK TIME:
1 cup*	10 minutes	0 minutes

*8 SERVINGS

This is my all-time favorite dressing and dipping sauce on or off the Whole30. The dates are a great way to get your kids to enjoy a Whole30-compatible sauce and/or help them transition away from traditional sweet sauces. I also enjoy this as an inexpensive yet delicious salad dressing that's full of healthy fats.

1 cup Homemade Mayo (page 253), or store-bought
3 tablespoons yellow mustard, plus more to taste
3 to 4 tablespoons Date Paste (page 269), to taste
Dairy-free milk, for adjusting consistency (optional)

1 In a blender, combine the mayo with 2 tablespoons of mustard and 3 tablespoons date paste and blend until smooth. You could also do this with an immersion blender. Taste and add the remaining mustard and/or date paste, if desired. If you'd prefer a thinner sauce or dressing, add the milk until your desired consistency is reached.

2 Store the dressing in a sealed container in the fridge for up to 2 weeks.

Homemade Ranch Dressing (with Cilantro Lime Ranch Variation)

WHOLE 30

MAKES:	PREP TIME:	COOK TIME:
1 to 1½ cups	10 minutes	0 minutes

A great sauce can go a long way in making meals come together, and this easy Homemade Ranch is a staple of our Whole30s. I often bring this to the opening potluck of my local Whole30 groups, and people insist that I start bottling and selling it. It's a mayo-based sauce, which means it's a great source of healthy fats. And it's also perfect for dipping and topping your salads. I have shared two ways to make it: one if you already have mayo on hand, and the dump ranch method for a super-easy one-step process. The Cilantro Lime Ranch variation is a must-have on-hand sauce for our family!

Method One: With Premade Mayo

1 cup Homemade Mayo (page 253), or store-bought
¼ to ½ cup full-fat coconut milk or other dairy-free milk
1 teaspoon garlic powder
1 teaspoon onion powder
1 teaspoon dried dill
1 teaspoon apple cider vinegar
Pinch each of ground salt and ground black pepper, or to taste

1 In a blender or medium bowl, combine the mayo, ¼ cup coconut milk, garlic powder, onion powder, dill, apple cider vinegar, and salt and pepper. Blend or whisk until smooth. Add more coconut milk, if desired, to adjust the consistency. Season with additional salt and pepper, if desired.

2 Store in a sealed container in the fridge for up to 2 weeks.

recipe continues

Method Two: Dump Ranch with Immersion Blender

1 cup extra-light-tasting olive oil
1 large egg
1 tablespoon lemon juice
¼ teaspoon salt
1 teaspoon garlic powder
1 teaspoon onion powder
1 teaspoon dried dill
1 teaspoon apple cider vinegar
Pinch of ground black pepper
Dairy-free milk of choice to desired thickness

1. In a container just slightly bigger than the head of your immersion blender—like a large-mouth mason jar—pour the oil and add the egg, lemon juice, salt, garlic powder, onion powder, dill, vinegar, and pepper. Let mixture sit for a few minutes so the egg can settle to the bottom.

2. Put the immersion blender into the mixture, positioning it right on top of the egg yolk. This placement is important. Wait 10 seconds. Turn on the immersion blender to high if your blender has speeds, holding it down at the bottom over the egg yolk. DO NOT MOVE for 10 seconds. After 10 seconds of blending on high at the bottom of the mixture, slowly pull up, still mixing, moving up and down slowly a few times through the whole mixture. The result should be creamy and thick.

3. Thin with a dairy-free milk to desired thickness.

4. Store in a sealed container in the fridge for up to 2 weeks.

Cilantro Lime Ranch Variation

After making ranch dressing as described, blend in 1 cup packed fresh cilantro, very finely chopped if mixing by hand, and 1 to 2 tablespoons lime juice, to taste.

Homemade Mayo and Chipotle Mayo

WHOLE 30 

MAKES:	PREP TIME:	COOK TIME:
1 cup	5 minutes	0 minutes

Note: Chipotle powder can be a little tricky to find. I find it at my local Supermercado or on Amazon. If you can't find it, you can use 1 canned chipotle pepper in adobo sauce blended into the mayo or 1 teaspoon+ of the adobe sauce stirred into the mayo. Just double-check your label; most canned chipotle peppers and adobo sauce are not Whole30-compatible.

I love that this homemade version of a store-bought staple is so affordable and easy to make. I can't recommend enough that you use an immersion blender for this because it yields the best consistency in barely any time. After ruining many batches of mayo with the slow pour method in my standing mixer, blender, and food processor, I bought an immersion blender, and it was a game changer! Make sure the olive oil you are using is labeled "extra-light-tasting," or the mayo will have a strong olive oil taste. The chipotle mayo has a fun kick and flavor that is so great in wraps and for dips.

FOR HOMEMADE MAYO:

1 large egg
1 cup extra-light-tasting olive oil
1 tablespoon fresh lemon or lime juice
⅛ teaspoon salt

FOR CHIPOTLE MAYO:

1 large egg
1 cup extra-light-tasting olive oil
1 tablespoon plus 1 teaspoon fresh lime juice
¼ teaspoon salt
½ to ¾ teaspoon chipotle powder
½ teaspoon garlic powder
¼ teaspoon paprika

1 If your immersion blender does not come with its own mixing container, find a jar that is bigger than the head of your blender. I use a wide-mouth mason jar.

recipe continues

2 In the container, crack the egg, follow with the oil, 1 tablespoon of lemon or lime juice, and salt. Let the ingredients settle for 1 to 2 minutes.

3 Place the head of the immersion blender directly on top of the egg yolk and blend on high, if your blender has speeds, for 10 to 15 seconds without moving your blender wand. While continuing to blend, slowly pull the blender up toward the top of the jar, slowly moving it up and down a few times. Voilà! The mayo should be emulsified, thick, and smooth.

4 **TO MAKE CHIPOTLE MAYO:** In a container, crack the egg, follow with the oil, lime juice, and salt. Let the ingredients settle for 1 to 2 minutes. Blend in ½ teaspoon of chipotle powder, plus the garlic powder and paprika. Adjust the seasoning by adding more chipotle powder and/or lime juice to taste.

5 Store the mayo in a sealed container in the fridge for up to 2 weeks.

Taco Seasoning Mix

WHOLE 30   	MAKES: 2½ tablespoons*	PREP TIME: 5 minutes	COOK TIME: 0 minutes

*2½ tablespoons = 1 mix

This homemade seasoning is such an easy, affordable way to make tacos happen without a lot of extra additives. All you need to do is stir in one batch of mix per pound of ground beef, cubed chicken*, or ground turkey* and cook until the meat is browned and cooked through. (*Use 1 tablespoon olive or avocado oil on the bottom of the pan to cook these leaner meats.) Once Whole30 taught me how to read my labels, I was shocked to learn that many taco seasoning packets have added sugar or gluten. But thanks to this recipe, I haven't bought a taco seasoning packet in ten years. I like to make it in a big batch to store in the pantry, remembering that 2½ tablespoons = 1 mix. This seasoning also works well to season fajitas.

1 tablespoon chili powder, or chipotle chili powder for more spice
1 tablespoon dehydrated minced onion
1 teaspoon ground cumin
½ teaspoon salt
½ teaspoon paprika
¼ to ½ teaspoon ground red pepper (optional for a kick)

In a small bowl, combine all of the ingredients if using immediately or in a small, sealed container or reusable zip-top bag if you plan to save it for later. The mix will keep in the pantry for up to 3 months.

Whole30 BBQ Sauce

WHOLE 30   	MAKES:	PREP TIME:	COOK TIME:
	2 cups (12 Servings)	10 minutes	10 minutes

BBQ sauce is my hubby's number-one favorite sauce. There are now several brands that offer delicious Whole30-compatible sauce, but at more than seven dollars a bottle, they don't fit well into a limited budget and can be difficult for some people to find in stores. This sauce costs less than one dollar per cup, and it's so flexible. Do you like a little more of a kick? Add the chili powder. Want a smoky flavor? Add the liquid smoke. I like Wright's brand liquid smoke, which you can find in the dressing aisle. Want it less or more sweet? Use less or more date paste.

1 (6-ounce) can tomato paste
2 to 4 tablespoons Date Paste (page 269)
1 tablespoon balsamic or apple cider vinegar
1 tablespoon yellow mustard
1 teaspoon salt
1 teaspoon garlic powder
½ teaspoon onion powder
¼ teaspoon ground black pepper
Optional: ½ teaspoon liquid smoke, for smoky flavor; ½ to 1 teaspoon chili powder, for a kick

1 In a blender or food processor, combine ¾ cup water, tomato paste, 2 tablespoons date paste, vinegar, mustard, salt, garlic powder, onion powder, pepper, liquid smoke (if using), and chili powder (if using) and blend until the mixture is smooth and all the ingredients are incorporated. Taste and adjust the seasonings to your preference. You can adjust the consistency by adding water, if needed.

2 In a medium saucepan over medium heat, bring the mixture to a boil. Reduce the heat to low and simmer for 10 minutes. Remove the pot from the heat and let the sauce cool completely. Store in a lidded container in the fridge for up to 3 weeks.

Nacho Cheese Sauce

WHOLE 30   

MAKES:	PREP TIME:	COOK TIME:
1 cup	5 minutes	10 minutes

Note: The thickness of this sauce will vary slightly depending on the thickness of your coconut milk. If the sauce does not thicken, mix an additional 1 teaspoon starch with 2 teaspoons cold water, creating a slurry. Add this slurry to the sauce and cook for 1 to 2 minutes more, until thickened.

My second son adores nachos and all their creamy, cheesy goodness, so I came up with this easy sauce to give him a dairy-free option. This sauce is excellent in my Tostones Nachos (page 76) or all by itself with tortilla chips, homemade Plantain Chips (page 164), or Tostones (page 224) as an appetizer or snack. You can also stir in some salsa or pico de gallo for an even more flavorful dip.

1 cup full-fat canned coconut milk
¼ cup nutritional yeast
1½ teaspoons potato or arrowroot starch, plus more if needed
½ teaspoon paprika
½ teaspoon salt
½ teaspoon garlic powder
¼ teaspoon chipotle powder

1 In a medium pot, cook the coconut milk, nutritional yeast, potato starch, paprika, salt, garlic powder, and chipotle powder over medium heat. Stir until the sauce thickens, 5 minutes, then remove the pot from the heat.

2 Store the sauce in a sealed container in the fridge for up to 2 weeks. Reheat before serving.

Flavor Boost Powder

WHOLE 30				MAKES: 6 tablespoons	PREP TIME: 10 minutes	COOK TIME: 0 minutes

This powder combines many of my favorite seasonings into one easy flavor boost. It only takes 10 minutes to mix and then is a simple scoop away from easily increasing the flavor of a variety of soups and entrées.

¼ cup nutritional yeast
2 teaspoons salt
2 teaspoons garlic powder
2 teaspoons onion powder
2 teaspoons dried basil
2 teaspoons dried oregano
1 teaspoon ground black pepper

In a food processor, combine all of the ingredients and process until well combined. Store in a sealed container for up to 3 months.

Creamy Apple Dressing

WHOLE 30

MAKES:	PREP TIME:	COOK TIME:
1½ cup	10 minutes	0 minutes

This sweet but tangy dressing is the perfect pairing for my Fuji Chicken Apple Salad (page 209) and Breakfast Salad (page 51). There's no egg involved, and it's easy to make in under 10 minutes. I just use whatever apple I have on hand and need to use up, usually a sweeter apple like a Fuji.

1 medium apple, peeled and cored
¾ cup extra-light-tasting olive oil
¼ cup white wine vinegar
3 tablespoons Date Paste (page 269)
1 tablespoon Dijon mustard
1 tablespoon lemon juice
Pinch of salt

In a blender or food processor, combine the apple, oil, vinegar, date paste, mustard, lemon juice, and salt and blend until completely smooth. Store in a sealed container in the fridge for up to 2 weeks. The dressing may separate over time; just give it a shake to recombine.

Homemade Nut Butter (with Chocolate Variation)

MAKES:	PREP TIME:	COOK TIME:
1 cup	15 minutes	0 minutes

Making your own nut butter is easy; it just takes a good food processor or blender and a little patience. I particularly love this recipe dressed up with chocolate. There is a brand of chocolate almond butter that we love and reach for on special occasions to smear on waffles and top with strawberries and coconut cream, but it is expensive and has a lot of refined sugar in it. I made this once in a pinch, and my boys had no idea it wasn't the sugar-laden store-bought brand! I prefer to make the chocolate variation with almonds/almond butter, but it's also delicious with hazelnuts (you need to remove the skins), peanuts, or cashews. You can also add all the ingredients besides the nuts to 1 cup store-bought nut butter for an easy chocolate nut butter hack.

TO MAKE NUT BUTTER:

2 cups raw almonds or other raw nut of choice
¼ teaspoon salt

TO MAKE CHOCOLATE VARIATION:

1 cup Homemade Nut Butter or store-bought
3 tablespoons cocoa powder
4 tablespoons coconut or maple sugar
3 to 5 tablespoons extra-light-tasting olive oil
1 teaspoon vanilla extract

1. Preheat the oven to 350°F.

2. Line a baking sheet with parchment paper and lay the nuts on the sheet in a single layer. Roast for 10 minutes, until fragrant and toasted.

3. In a blender or food processor, blend the nuts until completely smooth, 5 to 15 minutes, depending on the power of the processor. This will take some patience because you will need to repeatedly blend, stir, scrape down the sides, and blend some more. You will begin to think it will never turn into nut butter, but keep at it. If needed, you can add 1 to 2 tablespoons of oil, but it usually just needs more time. Add the salt once you've reached a creamy consistency.

4. Store in a sealed container in the pantry for up to 2 weeks.

CHOCOLATE VARIATION

To your nut butter in the blender, add the cocoa, sugar, 3 tablespoons oil, and vanilla and blend until combined. Add 1 to 2 tablespoons additional oil for a thinner consistency.

Berry Breakfast Syrup

MAKES:	PREP TIME:	COOK TIME:
1 cup	5 minutes	10 minutes

Note: The amount of sugar you'll need will depend on the fruit you're using. I find that 4 tablespoons are plenty for sweeter fruits like strawberries and blueberries, while 6 are better for more tart berries like raspberries and blackberries. I don't recommend using tapioca flour in this, as it makes the sauce too tacky. And you can make this recipe Keto by using another granulated sugar such as monk fruit in the same amount.

My boys love berry syrup made by a well-known jam and syrup brand. However, it is loaded with high-fructose corn syrup and sugar. This is our homemade version that works with so many flavors of fruit and lasts in the fridge for several weeks. I love that you can make it with fresh or frozen berries, which helps with cost saving. It's a great sauce to use any time you would normally reach for maple syrup.

2 cups fresh or frozen berries
4 to 6 tablespoons coconut or maple sugar
2 teaspoons arrowroot or potato starch
1 teaspoon vanilla extract

1 In a small pot, stir together the berries and sugar with ¼ cup water over medium heat. Bring the mixture to a boil and reduce to a simmer. Cook for 4 to 5 minutes, until the berries are soft.

2 Use a fine-mesh strainer to strain out any remaining pulp or seeds. Use a spatula to press through as much liquid as you can into the pot. Set aside any berries you strain out and use them as a fruit topping or in a smoothie.

3 In a small bowl, stir together the starch with 2 teaspoons water. Pour the starch mixture into the pot with the fruit liquid. Over medium heat, cook the mixture while stirring until it has thickened, 2 to 3 minutes. Remove the pot from the heat and stir in the vanilla. The sauce will thicken as it cools, and we prefer to eat it cool. Store in a sealed container in the fridge for up to 3 weeks.

Ranch Seasoning

WHOLE 30   	MAKES:	PREP TIME:	COOK TIME:
	2 tablespoons	10 minutes	0 minutes

Ranch is one of those universal flavors (almost) everyone loves. I developed this seasoning to bring ranch flavor to any dish. I especially love it on Bacon-Wrapped Ranch Chicken (page 93) and roasted nut mixes. Do yourself a favor by making a giant batch to sprinkle on everything—I quadruple this recipe and keep it in my pantry.

1 teaspoon garlic powder
1 teaspoon onion powder
1 teaspoon dried dill
1 teaspoon dried chives
1 teaspoon Italian seasoning
½ teaspoon salt
½ teaspoon ground black pepper

In a small bowl, combine all the ingredients. If you want a finer, more powder-like texture, you can pulse the mixture in a blender or food processor. Store the seasoning in a sealed container in the pantry for up to 3 months.

Ghee

WHOLE 30	MAKES:	PREP TIME:	COOK TIME:
	4 cups	0 minutes	Varies*

*COOK TIME: 2½ to 3 hours in slow cooker; 25 minutes for stovetop; 8 minutes in microwave

▸ **Note: Many bloggers recommend using unsalted butter to make ghee, as they find that salted butter can make the ghee salty. But I actually find ghee not salty enough and prefer using salted butter. Either will work.**

Ghee is a Whole30 and dairy-free cooking pantry staple. Although ghee has been popularized by Paleo, Keto, and Whole30 approaches in recent years, ghee originated in India and dates back to at least 1500 BCE. Ghee is butter that has had the milk solids removed, which makes it Whole30-compatible and shelf stable. Store-bought ghee is not always an option because it can be difficult to find and can be expensive. I also prefer the taste of homemade. I love making it in the slow cooker, which makes it harder to burn, though it's easy to do on the stovetop, too. I also included a microwave method that is my go-to in a time pinch, but it only does 1 stick of butter at a time.

1 pound butter (see Note)
Mason jar
Cheesecloth
Rubber band

1 **IF USING A SLOW COOKER:** Place the butter in the slow cooker and turn it to high. Only *partially* cover with the lid; do not seal the slow cooker as normal, and do not stir. Ghee is done when the surface is covered in light-brown foam with crispy edges and there are light-colored milk fat solids at the bottom. For me, that is about 2½ to 3 hours for 1 pound of butter in my 6-quart slow cooker.

2 **IF USING THE STOVETOP:** In a medium saucepan, melt the butter over medium heat. Once the butter has melted, reduce the heat to medium-low. The butter will begin to foam after about 6 to 7 minutes, which is when you should begin stirring occasionally. After roughly 20 minutes total, the butter will foam again and start making a popcorn-like sound as the milk solids begin to solidify. Turn off the heat, but leave the pan on the hot stove for 5 minutes more for the milk fats to finish solidifying.

3 **FOR THE MICROWAVE (MAKES ONLY 1 CUP):** Place 1 stick (½ cup) of butter in a glass container at least four times its size. I use a quart-size mason jar. Loosely cover the top of the container with a thin cloth to prevent splattering. Microwave for 3 minutes. Don't open the microwave. Leave the ghee in the closed microwave for 5 minutes. The milk solids should be separated and settled at the bottom of the container. Be careful taking container out of microwave—it will be hot!

4 **FOR ALL METHODS:** Once the milk fats have separated, cover the mason jar with a cheesecloth or thin, clean cloth, and secure it with a rubber band. Allow the cloth to sag about an inch into the jar to create a place for milk solids to collect. Ladle the ghee into the cheesecloth so the milk solids are strained out. Discard the milk solids and cover the jar.

5 The ghee can be stored in the pantry for 1 month or in the fridge for up to 3 months.

Pantry Marinara Sauce

WHOLE 30    

MAKES:	PREP TIME:	COOK TIME:
3 cups	5 minutes	10 minutes

Store-bought Whole30-compatible marinara sauce can be hard to find because most jarred versions have added sugar. Even if you can find one, it can be pricey, depending on which stores you have accessible to you. But it's so easy to make! This recipe focuses on using pantry staples like canned tomatoes and dried seasonings, but you are welcome to use fresh garlic and basil instead.

2 (15-ounce) cans petite diced tomatoes
1 (6-ounce) can tomato paste
½ cup water or chicken broth
1 tablespoon Flavor Boost Powder (page 258)
2 teaspoons dried basil
1 teaspoon dried oregano
1 teaspoon garlic powder
½ teaspoon salt
¼ teaspoon ground black pepper

1 In a medium saucepan, combine all the ingredients over medium heat. Bring the sauce to a boil, then reduce to a simmer for 7 to 8 minutes so the flavors can combine. At this point, the sauce is done, but you could puree the sauce in a blender or food processor if you want a smoother consistency.

2 Let the sauce cool and store in a sealed container in the fridge for up to 3 weeks or the freezer for up to 3 months.

Date Paste

WHOLE 30

MAKES:	PREP TIME:	COOK TIME:
½ cup	10 minutes	0 minutes

Date paste is a simple way to add a touch of sweetness to sauces and dressings without using highly refined sugars. Since it is just whole dates blended with water, it is Whole30-compatible. Blending it into a paste before mixing into a sauce will allow for a smoother result, without large chunks of date in your sauce.

1 cup packed pitted fresh dates (about 10 to 11 large dates)

½ cup very hot water

In a small bowl, combine the dates and hot water and let sit for 1 minute. I usually press them down into the water a bit to ensure all of them are soaking. In a blender or food processor, process the dates and all the liquid for 30 seconds, or until smooth. Store in a closed container in the fridge for up to 3 to 4 weeks.

9 CHAPTER

Desserts

Everything Cookies

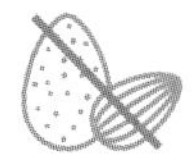

SERVES:	PREP TIME:	COOK TIME:
18*	15 minutes	10 minutes

*MAKES: 18 cookies

▾ **Note: I prefer the texture of these cookies with the almond flour. If you need a nut-free option, use ½ cup cassava flour + ½ cup + 2 tablespoons tapioca flour instead of the almond + tapioca flour.**

I have tried a lot of terrible Paleo cookie recipes, so I went on a quest to create a recipe that we actually loved. The key is in the palm shortening and maple sugar. You can swap them for ghee or coconut sugar, if that's more accessible to you, but I highly recommend the palm shortening and maple sugar. They make all the difference in the texture of these cookies. Don't skip freezing these before baking, as it helps them not spread too much as they bake. This recipe has so many options and possibilities, each one a favorite for a different family member.

¾ cup maple sugar
½ cup palm shortening
2 large egg yolks
1 teaspoon vanilla extract
1¼ cups almond flour (see Note)
¾ cup tapioca flour
1 teaspoon baking powder
¼ teaspoon salt
Mix-ins of choice (see Variations)

1 In a large bowl, combine the sugar, shortening, egg yolks, and vanilla and mix by hand until smooth. I don't recommend using a mixer as it whips more air into the dough and makes the cookies less soft, but you can use a mixer on low speed if needed.

2 Add the almond flour, tapioca flour, baking powder, and salt and stir again until everything is just combined. The dough will seem too dry at first, but keep stirring! Gently stir in any mix-ins or roll-in flavorings of choice (see Variations).

3 Line a plate or tray (one that will fit in your freezer) with parchment. Scoop 1½ tablespoons of dough and place on the parchment. Repeat with all the dough. Freeze for 15 minutes.

recipe continues

Freeze baked cookies in a sealed container for up to 3 months. Or you can freeze the scooped-out cookie dough balls in a single layer until frozen, then store in a sealed container for up to 3 months. For frozen cookie dough, follow baking instructions; no need to thaw!

4 Preheat the oven to 350°F. Line a baking pan with parchment paper. Place the frozen cookie dough onto the prepared pan, at least two inches apart.

5 Bake for 10 minutes, no longer, in order to keep the cookies nice and soft. Cool the cookies on a wire rack or the counter for 10 minutes before eating.

VARIATIONS:

Chocolate Chip Cookies

Stir in ⅓ to ½ cup white or semisweet dairy-free chocolate chips. We love a combination of chunks and mini chips.

Snickerdoodles

In a small bowl, combine ½ cup maple sugar and 1 tablespoon ground cinnamon. Roll each cookie in the cinnamon-sugar to coat before baking.

Chocolate Cookies

Use only 1 cup almond flour, no tapioca flour, and ⅓ cup cocoa plus any chocolate chips of choice mixed in. No need to freeze the chocolate cookie dough before baking.

Funfetti Cookies

Roll the cookies in ½ cup natural sprinkles of choice before freezing.

Chocolate Fondue

SERVES:	PREP TIME:	COOK TIME:
2	5 minutes	0 minutes

▸ **Note: The chocolate sauce will harden as it cools, thanks to the coconut oil, so keep it warm if you want to dip in it. This means that this also makes for a great magic shell–like ice cream topping.**

It's no secret that I love chocolate, so dipping things in it sounds delightful, and my kids also find it fun. You can get fancy with this by putting it in a chocolate fountain, which is great for parties or a fun family night.

3 tablespoons coconut oil, melted
3 tablespoons cocoa powder
2 tablespoons pure maple syrup
½ teaspoon mint extract (optional)
Optional: strawberries, gluten-free graham crackers or pretzels, marshmallows, for dipping

In a small bowl, whisk together the coconut oil, cocoa powder, maple syrup, and mint, if desired. Serve warm with dipping items of choice.

Paleo Fudgy Brownies

SERVES:	PREP TIME:	COOK TIME:
12*	20 minutes	30 to 35 minutes

*MAKES: 12 brownies

Note: You can use Ghee (page 266) or extra-light-tasting olive oil instead of the coconut oil. You can also use maple sugar or a sugar-free granulated sugar like monk fruit instead of the coconut sugar. And if you don't have a 9 x 13-inch baking pan, you can bake these in an 8-inch or 9-inch square pan for a deep-dish brownie (my favorite). You'll just need to bake 5 to 7 minutes more.

Brownies are my all-time favorite dessert. To me, they need to be thick and fuuudddgy. So, after many variations, I finally created a fudgy Paleo version that my family LOVES. These have only eight ingredients, are easy to make, and yield a large, family-size pan. They're delicious warm or at room temperature, and I highly recommend enjoying them topped with dairy-free ice cream.

2 cups semisweet dairy-free chocolate chips or mini chips
½ cup coconut oil (see Note)
1½ cups coconut sugar (see Note)
1 cup tapioca or arrowroot flour
3 large eggs, beaten
½ cup cocoa powder
1 tablespoon vanilla extract
½ teaspoon salt

1. Preheat the oven to 350°F. Line a 9 x 13-inch baking pan with parchment paper and set aside.

2. In a medium microwave-safe bowl or dish, combine the chocolate chips and coconut oil. Microwave for 1 minute then stir. The chocolate should be completely melted. If not, microwave for 30 seconds more and stir again. The mixture should be smooth and well combined.

3. Stir in the sugar, flour, eggs, cocoa powder, vanilla, and salt until combined.

4. Pour the brownie batter into the prepared pan and spread the mixture evenly. Bake for 30 to 35 minutes, until the brownies are just set. The middle should bounce back when touched. Be careful not to overbake or the brownies won't be fudgy.

Freeze cut individual brownies until frozen, then store all together in a sealed container.

Sugar Cookies

		SERVES: 18*	PREP TIME: 20 minutes	COOK TIME: 12 minutes

*MAKES: 18 cookies

These are wonderfully soft and reminiscent of packaged sugar cookies but with much improved ingredients.

Note: While I prefer the almond flour–tapioca flour combination, you can make these nut-free by using 1 cup cassava flour to replace both flours. This will result in a slightly smaller batch of cookies (about 12 cookies). And while you could use coconut sugar, I highly recommend investing in maple sugar, as I find that it has better flavor and makes for much better cookies.

Lay the frosted cookies in a single layer on a baking sheet and freeze before storing in a sealed container for 3-plus months.

FOR THE COOKIES:

1 cup maple sugar
½ cup palm shortening
2 large eggs
1 teaspoon vanilla extract
2½ cups almond flour (see Note)
½ cup tapioca flour
1 teaspoon baking powder
½ teaspoon baking soda
½ teaspoon salt

FOR THE FROSTING:

½ cup palm shortening
1 teaspoon vanilla extract
¼ cup honey
¼ cup maple sugar

1 Preheat the oven to 350°F. Line a baking sheet with parchment paper and set aside.

2 **MAKE THE COOKIES:** In a large bowl, use a spoon to cream together the sugar, shortening, eggs, and vanilla. Stir in the almond flour, tapioca flour, baking powder, baking soda, and salt and mix well.

3 Scoop small spoonfuls (about 1½ tablespoons each) of the batter onto the prepared baking sheet, spacing them about 2 inches apart to allow for spreading as they bake. Bake for 12 minutes, until the cookies have spread flat and the tops spring back when gently pressed.

4 **MAKE THE FROSTING:** While the cookies bake, make the frosting. In a small bowl, use a whisk or hand mixer to beat together the shortening, vanilla, honey, and sugar.

5 Once the cookies have cooled, spread the frosting over the tops. The cookies can be eaten immediately, but we highly prefer the texture of the frosting when the frosted cookies have chilled for at least 1 hour in the fridge.

Chocolate-Glazed Mini Donuts

SERVES:	PREP TIME:	COOK TIME:
15*	10 minutes	3 to 18 minutes**

*MAKES: 15 mini donuts
**COOK TIME: 3 to 18 minutes, depending on cooking pan and method

It's a rare person who doesn't love a good donut. These can be made in a donut pan or a mini donut maker, which is what I prefer. We love these on weekends and for special occasions. Don't have a donut maker or pan? This batter is also delicious made into cupcakes or mini cupcakes. I included two glaze options. This is one of the few times I prefer to use a traditional sugar in the dairy-free glaze; however, there is also a Paleo glaze option.

FOR THE DONUTS:

Optional: Nonstick cooking oil spray, if needed
¾ cup coconut or maple sugar
½ cup cassava flour or ½ cup tapioca flour + ⅓ cup almond flour
⅓ cup cocoa powder
1½ teaspoons baking powder
¼ teaspoon salt
3 large eggs
½ cup extra-light-tasting olive oil or melted coconut oil
1 teaspoon vanilla extract

FOR THE GLAZE:

DAIRY-FREE GLAZE

1¼ cups powdered sugar
¼ cup almond milk or other dairy-free milk
1 tablespoon melted Ghee (page 266), or store-bought
1 teaspoon vanilla extract

PALEO GLAZE

¼ cup coconut or maple sugar
¼ cup full-fat thick canned coconut milk
1 teaspoon vanilla extract

1 **MAKE THE DONUTS:** Preheat the oven to 350°F or plug in and preheat a mini donut maker. If using a donut or cupcake baking pan, spray with nonstick cooking oil or line with cupcake liners.

2 In a medium bowl, stir together the sugar, flour, cocoa powder, baking powder, and salt. Add the eggs, oil, and vanilla and stir until well combined.

3 Fill your donut baking pan or donut maker molds with the batter. That's about 1 heaping tablespoon full of batter for mini donut pans or molds and 2 heaping tablespoons full of batter for full-sized donut pans or molds. Bake for about 3 minutes in a mini donut maker, 13 minutes in a mini cupcake baking pan or mini donut pan, or 18 minutes in a full-sized donut baking pan or cupcake pan, until the tops of the donuts bounce back when pressed.

4 **WHILE THE DONUTS ARE COOKING, MAKE THE GLAZE:** In a medium bowl, whisk together all the glaze ingredients. When the donuts have finished baking, dip both sides in the glaze and transfer to a cooling rack or lined baking sheet. Refrigerate for 30 minutes to set, until glaze has hardened to the touch. You can speed this up by freezing the donuts for 10 minutes. Store in a sealed container in the fridge for up to 1 week.

Freeze in a single layer until frozen and then store in a sealed container in the freezer for up to 3 months.

Easy Chocolate Cream Pie

SERVES:	PREP TIME:	CHILL TIME:
8 to 12	15 minutes	3 to 4 hours

▾ **Note: For a nut-free crust option, blend 33 gluten-free chocolate sandwich–style cookies like Oreos in a food processor or blender until you get fine crumbs. Mix in ⅓ cup melted coconut oil or ghee until well combined. Press the mixture into a pie pan and make the filling as described below.**

I'm not the biggest fan of making pie because it's usually a lot of work and not enough chocolate is involved. But this pie is a chocolate lover's dream and it's easy to make—simple enough for a weeknight dessert but fancy enough to bring to Thanksgiving. This recipe works great as a whole pie or as mini single-serve pies, which are great for gatherings like baby showers or potlucks. The filling is also a luscious thick mousse on its own.

FOR THE CRUST:

1 cup whole walnuts (see Note)
1 cup whole unsalted almonds (see Note)
½ cup cocoa powder
¼ cup plus 2 tablespoons honey
1 teaspoon vanilla extract
Cooking spray (optional)

FOR THE MOUSSE FILLING:

1 (15-ounce) can coconut cream, at room temperature
⅓ cup cocoa powder
¼ cup honey
2 (0.25-ounce) packages or 1½ tablespoons gelatin
1 teaspoon vanilla extract

Optional: Whipped Coconut Cream (see next page) and small bits of chopped chocolate, for topping

1 **MAKE THE CRUST:** In a food processor, pulse the walnuts and almonds until they form a fine meal. Add the cocoa powder, honey, and vanilla and pulse until the mixture is well combined and holding together.

2 Press the crust mixture into a 9-inch pie pan. If making mini pies, press 2 tablespoons of mixture into the bottom of

recipe continues

12 muffin liners. I find the foil muffin liners come off the easiest. Spraying your hands with cooking spray can keep the crust mixture from sticking to your hands as you press it into the pan. Set the crust aside.

3 **MAKE THE FILLING:** In the bowl of a stand mixer fitted with the paddle attachment or in a medium bowl with a hand mixer, combine the coconut cream, cocoa, honey, gelatin, and vanilla. Mix until well combined.

4 Pour the filling into the prepared pie pan or muffin liners. If you are making mini pies, you will need about ¼ cup of filling per mini pie. Top with whipped coconut cream and chocolate bits, if using. Keep the pies in the refrigerator for 4 hours if making a whole pie or 3 hours if making mini pies. Serve cold and keep in the fridge for up to 1 week.

Cut into individual servings and store each in a sealed container in the freezer for up to 3 months.

Whipped Coconut Cream

1 (15-ounce) can chilled coconut cream
3 tablespoons honey
1 teaspoon vanilla extract

1 Open the can of coconut cream, drain, and set aside the nonsolid liquid. Use *only* the solid part of the canned coconut cream. In the bowl of a stand mixer or in a medium bowl with a hand mixer on high, combine all three ingredients for 30 seconds. The mixture will be drippy and not "fluffy" at this point because it is not yet chilled.

2 Pour the coconut cream mixture on top of the chocolate cream pie and chill as directed above. Or, if using the coconut cream separately, chill it in the fridge for at least 30 minutes to thicken. Store in the fridge for up to 2 weeks.

Paleo Ice Cream

SERVES:	PREP TIME:	FREEZE TIME:
2	5 minutes	20 to 25 minutes*

*FREEZE TIME: 20 to 50 minutes, depending on desired consistency

▾ **Note: Canned coconut cream must be used in the recipe, *not* just coconut milk. You will need 1 can. Make sure you use *only* the cream and *not* the liquid from the coconut cream can. I keep my coconut cream in the fridge because the cream only separates from the liquid when it's cold.**

When we switched to eating dairy-free, it was frustrating how the ice cream options were either terrible in texture or had a looong list of ingredients. Surely there had to be a simple, creamy option out there? Now there is, thanks to this recipe. This ice cream is incredibly creamy and tasty, yet the ingredients are simple, and it only takes 5 minutes of hands-on prep. This recipe is the sole reason I invested in an ice cream maker, and we haven't had store-bought ice cream since! This makes a small batch, so we always at least double it.

1 cup canned coconut cream (see Note)
½ cup almond or other dairy-free milk or creamer like nutpods
¼ cup honey
1½ teaspoons vanilla

1 In a blender, combine all the ingredients and blend until smooth. Blend at a low speed if you have a high-powered mixer like a Vitamix because high speeds will overmix the base and make it chunky. If this happens, there is no going back, so easy does it.

2 Pour the ice cream base into the ice cream maker. Turn on the ice cream maker and mix for 20 minutes, or until thick and creamy. This will result in a soft-serve texture, which we love! If you want something firmer and scoopable, put the ice cream in the freezer for 30 minutes.

3 Serve right out of the freezer and enjoy! Store in a sealed container in the freezer for up to 3 months.

recipe continues

VARIATIONS

Mint Chip Ice Cream

Use 1½ teaspoons mint extract instead of the vanilla. Once the ice cream is starting to thicken in the ice cream maker, add ⅓ cup dairy-free mini chips.

Cookies and Cream

Add 1 cup crushed gluten-free Oreos into the vanilla ice cream batter once the ice cream is starting to thicken in the ice cream maker.

Chocolate Ice Cream

Increase the honey to ½ cup and add ⅓ cup cocoa to the blender before blending.

Gingersnap Cookies

SERVES:	PREP TIME:	COOK TIME:
18*	25 minutes	8 to 10 minutes

*MAKES: 18 cookies

In college, I had the incredible opportunity to be head of the BYU Wellness Program for 5,000+ BYU faculty and staff. We had regular Fun Walks to encourage employees to get out and move their bodies, and they wrapped up with water, fruit, and these cookies. Don't get me wrong, cookies aren't a health food. These are a treat, but I'm pretty sure many staff members came out just for these gingersnaps, and they bring back a lot of great memories for me. Here is a gluten-free, Paleo version of them!

1 cup coconut sugar
¼ cup Ghee (page 266), melted, or store-bought
1 large egg
2 tablespoons molasses
¾ cup plus 2 tablespoons cassava flour
1 teaspoon baking powder
¼ teaspoon salt
½ teaspoon ground cinnamon
¼ teaspoon ground cloves
¼ teaspoon ground ginger

1 Preheat the oven to 350°F. Line a baking sheet with parchment paper and set aside.

2 In a medium bowl, combine ¾ cup of coconut sugar with the ghee, egg, and molasses. Stir until well combined. Add the flour, baking powder, and spices to the wet mixture and stir until well combined.

3 Place the remaining ¼ cup coconut sugar on a plate. To make the cookies, scoop out the dough 1 tablespoon at a time. Roll each scoop into a ball and then roll it in the remaining sugar to coat. Freeze the dough balls for 20 minutes.

4 After freezing, arrange the dough balls on the lined baking sheet, spacing them at least 2 inches apart.

5 Bake for 8 to 10 minutes, until the centers are just set. Don't overbake these, or they will lose their chewy texture!

Freeze the cookies in a single layer, then store them in a sealed container for up to 6 months.

Paleo Milkshakes

SERVES:	PREP TIME:	COOK TIME:
1	5 minutes	0 minutes

Milkshakes are my second son's favorite dessert. When we have our annual back-to-school "Yes Day," you bet there is a milkshake or two on his list every time. My Paleo Ice Cream (page 289) calls for minimal ingredients, so the sky's the limit on the mix-ins and flavorings. Adjust the milk amount to your desired thickness. We like it thick, so start with the ¼ cup milk and go from there. All of these are nut-free except the Peanut Butter Milkshake.

1½ cups vanilla Paleo Ice Cream (page 289)
¼ cup almond milk or other dairy-free milk
1 cup mix-ins of choice (see below)

In a blender, combine the ice cream and almond milk and pulse until just blended. Add the mix-ins of choice and pulse until incorporated. Don't overblend or the mix-ins will lose their texture and the milkshake will be thin.

Oreo Milkshake

Add 6 gluten-free Oreos or similar chocolate sandwich-type cookies. You can also add ½ teaspoon mint extract for a Mint Oreo Milkshake!

Georgia Mud Fudge Milkshake

Use chocolate ice cream as your base and add one of my Paleo Fudgy Brownies (page 278), chopped into small pieces, plus ¼ cup chopped walnuts.

Raspberry Milkshake

Add ½ cup frozen or fresh raspberries or ¼ cup of my raspberry Berry Breakfast Syrup (page 264). Also excellent with chocolate chips or brownie bits!

Peanut Butter Milkshake

Add ¼ cup peanut butter with 2 or 3 of my homemade Chocolate Nut (or Seed) Butter Cups (page 303).

Oreo Brownie Cheesecake

SERVES:	PREP TIME:	CHILL TIME:
12	40 minutes*	3 hours

*PREP TIME: 20 minutes + 20 minutes for Paleo Fudgy Brownies

Note: When making the Paleo Fudgy Brownies for this recipe, use extra-light-tasting olive oil instead of coconut oil because coconut oil will harden when it gets cold. You will need only a half batch cooked in a 9-inch springform pan, an 8 x 8-inch square pan, or a 9 x 9-inch square pan. Be sure to line the pan with parchment paper—just the bottom of the springform but the entire pan if using a square pan. You can cook the other half of the batter in another square pan at the same time or as brownie bites for 15 minutes in a prepared muffin tin. Bake as you otherwise would, but give yourself time to let the brownies cool before incorporating them into the cheesecake mixture. If you're in a hurry, you can put the whole pan of baked brownies in the freezer for 30 minutes to cool before adding the cheesecake layer.

Oreo Cheesecake from a well-known cheesecake restaurant was my very favorite dessert, which says a lot for a foodie who adores desserts. I had it every year for my birthday, and it was so many of my favorite things in one. I started to notice that the week after having that cheesecake, even while eating an otherwise Paleo diet, my previously clear face would break out with acne and I'd feel super sluggish with brain fog. As someone who has always struggled with my skin, that cheesecake indulgence became less and less worth it. I knew this one had to be re-created, and it has been our family's birthday dessert of choice since creation. Buckle up! This one is a showstopper!

½ batch Paleo Fudgy Brownies recipe (page 278, see Note)
1 (16-ounce) container dairy-free cream cheese
½ cup full-fat coconut milk or other dairy-free milk
½ cup honey
3 (0.25-ounce) packets or 2 tablespoons gelatin
1 tablespoon vanilla extract
1 (13-ounce) package gluten-free chocolate sandwich-style cookies (approximately 33 cookies)
Optional: ½ cup melted dairy-free chocolate chips, Whipped Coconut Cream (page 288), additional whole cookies, for topping

1 In a blender, combine the cream cheese, milk, honey, gelatin, and vanilla and blend until well combined.

2 Smash the cookies into large chunks. I prefer to do this in a reusable zip-top bag with a kitchen mallet versus a food processor because the machine makes the pieces too small.

recipe continues

3 Gently fold half the cookie chunks into the cream cheese mixture. Be careful not to overmix, or your cheesecake will turn gray. Pour the batter on top of the cooled brownie, spreading evenly.

4 Sprinkle the remaining cookie chunks over the top. Gently press them into the cream cheese layer.

5 Chill the cheesecake for at least 3 hours, or up to overnight. Enjoy with optional toppings such as a melted chocolate chip sauce, Whipped Coconut Cream, or additional whole cookies.

Cut the cheesecake into individual servings and freeze each in a sealed container for up to 3 months.

Apple Fries with Cheesecake Dip

SERVES:	PREP TIME:	COOK TIME:
4	20 minutes	5 to 7 minutes

There is a Southern California theme park that is known for their apple fries: think apple pie as a finger food. This is my version, which goes from "tasty" to "wow" when you add the cheesecake-inspired dip. This fruit-based dessert is fun and easy, and it's also a kid favorite in our home. The dip is excellent served separately with things like strawberries, raw apple slices, vanilla wafers, and so on. I use my Paleo Vanilla Wafers (page 178) for the breading to keep this recipe affordable and accessible, but you can also use an equal amount of store-bought gluten-free graham cracker or wafer crumbs. These can be made in the oven or air fryer.

FOR THE APPLE FRIES:

3 large apples, any type
⅓ cup tapioca, arrowroot, or potato starch or flour
2 large eggs
1½ cups vanilla wafer crumbs (about ½ batch of the Paleo Vanilla Wafers, page 178)
⅓ cup maple or coconut sugar
Cooking oil spray, if air frying

FOR THE CHEESECAKE DIP:

1 (8-ounce) container dairy-free cream cheese
½ cup maple or coconut sugar
1 teaspoon vanilla extract

1. **MAKE THE APPLE FRIES:** If using the oven, preheat to 375°F. Line a baking sheet with parchment paper and set aside.

2. Cut the apples into wedges or fry shapes. No need to peel them.

recipe continues

3 In a medium bowl, place the starch or flour. In another medium bowl, beat the eggs. Toss the apples with the starch or flour, shaking off any excess before tossing them with the egg. Place the dredged apples in a colander and drain well. Give the colander a shake to remove any excess egg. I like this method because it saves you from having to dip each individual piece of apple (you're welcome).

4 In a medium bowl, combine the wafer crumbs and sugar. Add the apples and stir gently until all apples are coated. You can also do this in a large reusable bag, sealing and then shaking.

5 **IF BAKING:** Place the apple slices on the prepared baking sheet and bake for 10 minutes, until golden. Let the apples cool on the pan for 10 minutes; the coating will get crispier as it cools.

Spray the basket generously with cooking spray. Air fry at 350°F for 8 minutes, stirring halfway through. The apples should be golden and crispy.

6 **MAKE THE DIP:** In a stand mixer fitted with the paddle attachment or a hand mixer, combine the cream cheese, sugar, and vanilla. Mix until well combined and refrigerate until the apples are ready.

Chocolate Nut (or Seed) Butter Cups

SERVES:	PREP TIME:	FREEZE TIME:
12*	15 minutes	15 minutes

*MAKES: 12 cups

Peanut butter cups are a big favorite in our family. It's like those two flavors, chocolate and peanut butter, were just meant to be together. The ingredients in the store-bought ones are a mile long and often include dairy. However, these handheld treats hit the same spot with much better ingredients. My family loves these made with peanut butter, but they work just as well with your favorite nut or nut-free butter of choice.

½ cup nut or seed butter of your choice
3 tablespoons honey
¼ cup plus 1 tablespoon coconut oil, melted
1½ cups dairy-free chocolate mini chips
Muffin liners (foil ones work best)
Cooking spray

1 In a medium bowl, stir together the nut or seed butter, honey, and ¼ cup of coconut oil. Set aside.

2 In a small saucepan over low heat, combine the chocolate chips with remaining 1 tablespoon coconut oil, stirring constantly for 2 to 3 minutes, until chocolate has melted.

3 Line a muffin tin with muffin liners or spray the wells generously with cooking spray. A mini muffin tin will work, too. If making regular-size nut butter cups, pour ½ tablespoon melted chocolate in the bottom of each well. For mini nut butter cups, use 1 teaspoon chocolate. Spread the chocolate with the back of a spoon to coat the muffin well. Freeze until the chocolate has set, 5 to 10 minutes.

4 Top the chilled chocolate with 1 tablespoon nut or seed butter mixture for regular peanut butter cups, 1 teaspoon for mini. Freeze again until set, 10 to 15 minutes.

5 Top the nut or seed butter layer with another ½ tablespoon chocolate for regular peanut butter cups or 1 teaspoon for mini. Freeze one last time until set, 5 to 10 minutes. Store the cups in the fridge for up to 2 weeks or in the freezer for up to 3 months.

Paleo Ice Pops

SERVES:	PREP TIME:	FREEZE TIME:
8*	10 minutes	1 to 2 hours

*MAKES: 8 ice pops

▾ **Note: Instead of adding a sweetener to the strawberry ice pops, I use the sweetness of thawed juice concentrate. I recommend using a juice that is sweet like apple, or we also love using an apple-strawberry or apple-raspberry juice, if you can find it.**

▸ **Tip: The Chocolate Paleo Pudding (page 181) also freezes well as healthy fudge pops, as does the Pink Starburst Smoothie (page 54).**

These can be kept in the freezer for up to 1 month.

We live in Northern California, where it is over 90°F outside during much of the summer. There are many days when a light, cool treat really hits the spot, and these ice pops are healthy remakes of the ones we used to love to grab from the store. They are so easy to make, low on added sugar, and popular with everyone in the neighborhood.

FOR STRAWBERRY ICE POPS:

4 cups thawed frozen strawberries
1 cup thawed frozen juice concentrate (see Note)

FOR ORANGE CREAM ICE POPS:

2 cups orange juice
1 cup full-fat coconut milk
⅓ cup honey
1 teaspoon vanilla extract

1 **TO MAKE THE STRAWBERRY ICE POPS:** In a blender or food processor, blend the strawberries and juice concentrate until just combined. I like the mixture to have some bigger chunks of strawberries. Pour the base into ice pop molds and freeze 1 to 2 hours, depending on the size of your molds.

2 **TO MAKE THE ORANGE CREAM ICE POPS:** In a blender, blend the juice, coconut milk, honey, and vanilla until well combined, 1 to 2 minutes. For the best texture, add the base mixture to an ice cream maker for 10 minutes, until it almost soft serve-like in texture. Alternatively, add the mixture directly to your ice pop molds. Freeze 1 to 2 hours, depending on the size of your molds.

Chocolate-Coated Ice Cream Sandwiches

SERVES:	PREP TIME:	COOK TIME:	FREEZE TIME:
6*	20 minutes	10 to 12 minutes	1½ hours

*MAKES: 6 sandwiches

My family's favorite dessert growing up was chocolate-covered oatmeal ice cream sandwiches. I can't tell you the number of good memories wrapped up in those little sandwiches, and I knew I had to re-create a gluten-free, dairy-free version. This is our family favorite pairing of gluten-free oatmeal cookies and vanilla ice cream, but there are so many possibilities out there, like using chocolate cookies with mint chip ice cream. Get creative!

Note: To make these ice cream sandwiches nut-free, use cookies that are nut-free, such as the nut-free version of my Everything Cookies (page 272).

3 cups vanilla Paleo Ice Cream (page 289), or store-bought
12 Gluten-Free Oatmeal Cookies, or cookies of your choice (make sure they're uniform in size)
12 ounces dairy-free chocolate chips or mini chips
2 tablespoons coconut oil (optional)

GLUTEN-FREE OATMEAL COOKIES (see Note):

½ cup palm shortening
¾ cup maple sugar
2 egg yolks
1 teaspoon vanilla extract
¾ cup old-fashioned oats
½ cup tapioca flour
¾ cup almond flour
1 teaspoon baking powder
¼ teaspoon salt

1 **TO MAKE THE COOKIES:** Preheat the oven to 350°F and line a baking sheet with parchment paper.

2 In a medium bowl, combine the shortening, sugar, egg yolks, and vanilla with a mixer until smooth.

3 Add the dry ingredients and mix again until just combined. It will seem too dry at first, but keep stirring.

4 Roll 1½ tablespoons of dough into a ball and place on the lined baking sheet. Repeat with all the dough, spacing the dough balls at least 2 inches apart.

recipe continues

5 Bake for 10 to 12 minutes. Cook on a cooling rack or on the counter for at least 10 minutes before making the sandwiches.

6 **TO MAKE THE SANDWICHES:** Scoop ½ cup ice cream on top of each of 6 cookies. Sandwich the ice cream with the remaining 6 cookies. Freeze until the ice cream is set (about 1 hour).

7 In a small heat-proof bowl, microwave the chocolate chips and coconut oil (if using) for 1 minute. Stir and microwave for 30 seconds more. Stir again and repeat as needed if the chocolate chips haven't completely melted. Be careful; there's no coming back from burnt chocolate. Alternatively, you can melt the chocolate in a medium pot on the stove on low heat, stirring constantly until melted.

8 Dip the edges of each sandwich in the chocolate. Freeze again until the chocolate has set, 30 minutes.

Wrap the sandwiches individually with plastic wrap and then store them in the freezer in a sealed container for up to 3 months.

Pineapple Whip

   	SERVES: 2	PREP TIME: 10 minutes	COOK TIME: 0 minutes

▾ Note: I prefer using coconut milk in this because of its rich texture, but you can use whatever dairy-free milk works for your family. You can also use 1 banana instead of the honey for sweetness.

Many who've been to the theme park known as the "Happiest Place on Earth" have had a creamy but light pineapple whip dessert. This copycat version takes only 10 minutes, with fantastic ingredients that make this treat a no-brainer YES to enjoy.

4 cups frozen pineapple
½ cup dairy-free milk of choice (see Note)
¼ cup honey (see Note)
1 teaspoon vanilla extract

In a blender or food processor, combine the pineapple, milk, honey, and vanilla and blend until completely smooth. The mixture will be thick—don't be tempted to add more milk, or the whip will be too thin. Enjoy immediately for a soft-serve texture. For a thicker texture, transfer the mixture to an ice cream maker, and mix for 5 minutes or freeze the mixture for 30 minutes before enjoying. If it's been in the freezer for more than 30 minutes, let it sit out on the counter for 20 to 30 minutes to thaw before scooping.

Churro Bites

		SERVES: 36*	PREP TIME: 25 minutes	COOK TIME: 12 minutes

*MAKES: 36 bites

▸ **Note: This recipe only uses half a batch of my All-Purpose Dough, but I still make a full batch and just use the other half to make some rolls or pizza crust for dinner. I prefer to roll them in maple sugar because it is less gritty than coconut sugar.**

Churros date back to the sixteenth century. It's unknown whether the Spanish explorers who brought them to the New World got them from Portuguese sailors who adapted a fried flour stick in Northern China called "youtiao" to make it a sweet dessert, or from nomadic Spanish shepherds who named it after a type of sheep called the "Navajo-Churro" whose horns resemble a churro.

I made these out of curiosity after my son came home raving about the churro bites he had at a local café. I suspected they could be easily made with my Paleo All-Purpose Dough, and I was right. My kids and I all agreed these had to be in the cookbook!

½ batch Paleo All-Purpose Dough (page 236)
¾ cup maple or coconut sugar
1½ tablespoons ground cinnamon
½ cup coconut oil
Optional: Glaze (page 284), or store-bought frosting, for topping

1 Pinch off and roll the dough into 36 quarter-size balls. Set aside.

2 In a small bowl, combine the sugar and cinnamon.

3 In a medium pot, melt the coconut oil over medium heat. Once the oil is hot, add the dough balls (I do 6 at a time), and cook the dough in batches. Cook for 1 minute on each side, until golden. Watch them carefully; they cook fast!

4 Once both sides are cooked, remove the churro bites from the oil and put them straight into the cinnamon and sugar mixture. This will help the mixture stick to the churro bite. Roll each bite in the cinnamon-sugar mixture until coated and then set aside on a plate.

5 Repeat the cooking and rolling process with all the remaining dough.

6 If using glaze, drizzle on top. If using store-bought frosting, melt and then drizzle it.

Freeze the cooked churro bites in a single layer until frozen. Then store in a sealed container for up to 3 months. If using icing, freeze that separately, topping the bites just before eating. These warm great in an air fryer at 350°F for 5 minutes from the freezer!

Acknowledgments

MATT—There is no other name that belongs at the top of this list. We have been married for twenty years, and I have lived more of my life with you than without you. You are my eternal cheerleader, supporter, love, and best friend. Thank you for believing in me before I did, for the *many* sacrifices to chase down this big dream, and for the ridiculous number of dishes you tackled so I could create.

MELISSA—Wow, there are so many ways in which this book literally wouldn't be here without you. Your vision and leadership created a program that has done such beautiful things for me and my family, and I will probably get teary-eyed around every Friendsgiving table talking about it. Thank you for inspiring me to be better in countless areas and for being a powerful role model to me. Thank you for welcoming me to the Whole30 team, which feels like family, and for fiercely having my back.

SARAH AND THE MARINER BOOKS TEAM—Thank you for your belief in me and your enthusiasm for this book from the start. You have been incredibly supportive and so wonderful to work with.

AUBREY—My favorite sister. You have always been there in all the big and little moments of my life, but you really took the cake (ha-ha) with this one. Thank you for letting me brainstorm with you, talk your ear off about all things cookbook for months, and the *incredible* countless hours of recipe testing. I adore you and am so grateful we have each other.

TO MY BOYS—For being the best recipe testers, even when you pretended it wasn't great yet just so I would make it again. Thank you for giving me space to fulfill this dream, and I can't wait to watch you grow and chase down your own dreams.

LEEANNA—Thank you for never putting your pom-poms down and for the decades of love and late-night talks. You are such a blessing to my life, and your support during this cookbook was no exception.

TO THE WHOLE30 TEAM: Steph G., Alyssa, Liilu, Chelsea, Steph K., Mikey, Bill, Shanyn, Shannon, Shanna, Erica, Lindsay, Melissa S., Perla, and Ashley—Thank you for all the incredible support, feedback, and faith you gave me while I was creating this. I love our work family.

TO MY PARENTS—Thank you for your love and for teaching me to work hard.

LACEY—Thank you for bailing me out of so many camera hang-ups, generously loaning me your gear, letting me pick your photography brain, and capturing the beautiful family photos.

TO THE WHOLE30 COACHES: Thank you for the beautiful support and community. I grow from you daily and am honored to be among you.

TO MY SQUAD, STACEY, ROSALIE, AND TIFFANY—I don't know how I would survive raising kids without our chats and adventures. Thanks for the laughs until my cheeks hurt, adventures we will never forget, memes that bring a smile to my day, and being the village for my kids.

Index

NOTE: Page references in *italics* indicate photos of recipes.

U

V

W

About the Author

AUTUMN MICHAELIS is the Whole30 Coaching Manager and an Advanced Level Whole30 Certified Coach. She is also an ACSM Certified Exercise Physiologist, and holds a B.S. in Exercise Science from BYU. Exercise was her first love, but nutrition has become her passion, as she has seen personally and in so many others the powerful ways in which food directly affects our health.

Autumn is a home cook for home cooks who want delicious healthy food to feel approachable and simple. Her family of seven has eaten Paleo since 2017 and she wanted to provide more Whole30 and Paleo family-friendly recipes and resources.

She is a mom to five boys ages eight to eighteen and loves adventuring, dancing, and developing whole-food recipes on her blog *Whole Food For 7*. She lives just north of Sacramento, CA.